Greek Art and Literature
700-530 BC

De Carle Lectures, 1959

Methuen:

From Mycenae to Homer
Greek Theatre Production

Athlone Press:

Art and Literature in fourth century Athens

GREEK ART
AND LITERATURE
700-530 BC

The Beginnings
of Modern Civilization

T. B. L. WEBSTER

Professor of Greek
in the University of London

LONDON
METHUEN & CO. LTD
36 ESSEX STREET · STRAND · WC2

First published 1959

© 1959 *by the University of Otago Press*

Printed in New Zealand by
John McIndoe Ltd, Dunedin

TO MY FRIENDS
IN THE
UNIVERSITY OF OTAGO

Acknowledgements

ACKNOWLEDGEMENTS are due to the following for photographs and permission to publish: Professor H. Bloesch, M. P. Courbin, Dr. Chr. Karouzos, Professors E. Kunze, H. Möbius, as well as to the American School, the French School, and the German Archaeological Institute at Athens, the National Museum in Athens, the Musée Communal at Boulogne, the Otago Museum at Dunedin, the British Museum in London, the Louvre in Paris, the Wagner Museum in Würzburg and the Verlag F. Bruckmann KG.

I am very grateful to my wife for reading through my manuscript. For the errors that remain I am responsible. Professor G. R. Manton and Mr. P. Havard-Williams, editor of the University of Otago Press, saw the book through the galley-proof stage and I am extremely indebted to them and to the printers for making my difficult manuscript look so attractive.

T. B. L. WEBSTER

September, 1958

The de Carle Lectures

The de Carle lectures were founded in 1946 as the result of a bequest to the University of Otago by Miss Edith Isabelle de Carle. The lectures are given by visiting lecturers on subjects within the range of the Faculty of Arts and Music.

1948   The Right Honourable Lord Beveridge

1949   Sir Peter Buck, K.C.M.G.

1954   Professor Roy Daniells

1959   Professor Thomas Bertram Lonsdale Webster

Contents

Plates

(Numbers in brackets refer to the List of Monuments)

1 ATTIC GEOMETRIC PITCHER 760/40. Athens, National Museum 226

Photograph: German Archaeological Institute

2 PARIAN AMPHORA (88), DEER 660/50. Stockholm, National Museum 1

Photograph: Stockholm National Museum

3 ARGIVE KRATER (66), ODYSSEUS AND POLYPHEMOS 675/50. Argos Museum

Photograph: French School of Athens

4 MELIAN AMPHORA (89), APOLLO ARRIVING IN DELOS 660/50. Athens, National Museum 911

From E. Pfuhl, *Malerei und Zeichnung III*, fig. 108

5 CRETAN LIMESTONE STATUE (9) 640/30. Paris, Louvre 3098

Photograph: Louvre photographic archives

6 IONIAN MARBLE HEAD (25) 550 *circa*. London, British Museum, B 91

Photograph: British Museum

7 ATTIC MARBLE STATUE (2), FROM SOUNION 600 *circa*. Athens, National Museum 2720

Photograph: German Archaeological Institute

8 ATTIC MARBLE STATUE (7), KROISOS 540/30. Athens, National Museum 3851

Photograph: German Archaeological Institute

Abbreviations

(other than those adopted by *L'Année Philologique*)

A.B.L.	= C.H.E. Haspels, *Attic Black-figured Lekythoi*, Paris, 1936.
A.B.V.	= J. D. Beazley, *Attic Black-figure Vase-painters*, Oxford, 1956.
A.M.S.	= H. G. H. Payne and G. M. Young, *Archaic Marble Sculpture from the Acropolis*,London, 1936.
Anderson	= J. K. Anderson, *Greek Vases in the Otago Museum*, Dunedin, 1955.
Bowra	= C. M. Bowra, *Greek Lyric Poetry*, Oxford, 1936.
C.V.	= *Corpus Vasorum Antiquorum*.
D.	= E. Diehl, *Anthologia Lyrica*, Leipzig, 1935-52.
D.B.F.	= J. D. Beazley, *Development of Attic Black-figure*, Berkeley, 1951.
D.P.	= H. Fränkel, *Dichtung und Philosophie des frühen Griechentums*, New York, 1951.
Dunbabin (1957)	= T. J. Dunbabin, *The Greeks and their Eastern Neighbours*, Hellenic Society, Supplementary Paper, no. 8 (1957).
G.A.L.	= T. B. L. Webster, *Greek Art and Literature*, 530-400, Oxford, 1939.
G.H.I.	= M. N. Tod, *Greek Historical Inscriptions*, I, Oxford, 1946.
G.T.P.	= T. B. L. Webster, *Greek Theatre Production*, Methuen, 1956.
Karo	= G. Karo, *Greek Personality in Archaic Sculpture*, Harvard, 1948.
K.R.	= G. S. Kirk and J. E. Raven, *The Presocratic philosophers*, Cambridge, 1957.
L.	= F. Lasserre, *Archiloque*, Paris, 1958.
Lane	= A. Lane, *Greek Pottery*, London, 1947.
Lasserre	= F. Lasserre, *Les Epodes d'Archiloque*, Paris, 1950.
Lippold	= G. Lippold, *Griechische Plastik* (Iwan Müller Handbuch, VI, 5), Munich, 1950.

L.-P.   = E. Lobel and D. L. Page, *Poetarum Lesbiorum fragmenta*, Oxford, 1955.

M.H.   = T. B. L. Webster, *From Mycenae to Homer*, Methuen, 1958.

NC.   = H. G. H. Payne, *Necrocorinthia*, Oxford, 1928.

Page   = D. L. Page, *Sappho and Alcaeus*, Oxford, 1955.

Peek   = W. Peek, *Griechische Versinschriften*, Berlin, 1955.

Pfuhl   = E. Pfuhl, *Malerei und Zeichnung der Griechen*, Munich, 1923.

Picard   = C. Picard, *Manuel d'archéologie Grecque, la Sculpture*, I, Paris, 1935.

Richter   = G. M. A. Richter, *Archaic Greek Art*, New York, 1949.

Rumpf   = A. Rumpf, *Malerei und Zeichnung* (Iwan Müller Handbuch, VI, 6), Munich, 1953.

VS.   = H. Diels and W. Franz, *Fragmente der Vorsokratiker*, Berlin, 1934.

W.F.   = H. Fränkel, *Wege und Formen frühgriechischen Denkens*, Munich, 1955.

Chronological Table of Authors
and Works Mentioned

(Numbers refer to List of Monuments)

Before 700. Homer, *Iliad* and *Odyssey*. Eumelos of Corinth. *Hymn to Apollo*. Hesiod.

Vases: Attic Geometric (fig. 1).

700-675. Terpander.

Sculpture: Tiryns Gorgon (8), Mantiklos Apollo (1), satyr vase from Samos (20).

Vases: Early Proto-Attic (30-32), Early Protocorinthian (64).

675-650. Archilochos, Kallinos, Tyrtaios, Aristeas.

Sculpture: Artemis of Nikandre (19).

Vases: Middle Proto-Attic (33-37), middle Protocorinthian (65), Argive Orientalizing (66, fig. 3), Cycladic Orientalizing (88-90, fig. 2, 4), Aristonophos krater (102).

650-625. Alkman.

Sculpture: Lady of Auxerre (9, fig. 5).

Vases: Late Proto-Attic (38), late Protocorinthian (67), late Cycladic (91), East Greek wild goat style.

625-600. Arion, Semonides of Amorgos, Mimnermos of Kolophon.

Sculpture: Apollo of Sounion (2, fig. 7), New York kouros (3), Amazon relief (4), Arcadian goats (10), Argive shield bands (11).

Vases: Nessos ptr. etc. (39-42), early Corinthian (68-9).

600-575. Solon, Sappho, Alkaios, Thales, Stesichoros.

Sculpture: Kleobis (12), Corcyra pediments (13), Sikyonian treasury (14), Samian goat man (21),
metopes of Foce da Sele (29).

Vases: KY painter (43), Sophilos (44-5), Middle Corinthian (70-79, fig. 11), East Greek plates
(92-3).

575-550. Anaximander.

Sculpture: Berlin goddess (5), Argive shieldbands (15-17),
Ortheia masks (18), Hera of Cheramyes (22),
Anaximander kore (23), earlier Branchidai
statues.

Vases: Kleitias (46-7), Burgon group (48-9), Tyrrhenian
(50-51), Lydos (52), Heidelberg ptr. etc.
(53-56, fig. 12), late Corinthian (80-84),
Laconian (85-6).

550-525. Thespis, Pherekydes of Syros, Anaximenes, Hipponax, Ibykos, Anakreon, Xenophanes, Pythagoras.

Sculpture: Kore 679 (6), Kroisos (7, fig. 8), Nike of Delos
(24), Ephesos head (25, fig. 6), Chares (26),
Aiakes (27), Samian satyr mask (28).

Vases: Exekias etc. (57-60, fig. 13, 10), Amasis painter
(61), Antimenes painter (62), Chalkidian
(87, fig. 9), Clazomenian (94), Caeretan
hydriae (96-101, fig. 15), Campana dinoi
(103).

525-500. Herakleitos, Simonides, Hekataios.

Vases: Leagros group (63, fig. 14), Fikellura (95).

Introduction

I MUST first express my gratitude to the University of Otago for inviting me to give these de Carle lectures. The invitation allows me to finish off a piece of work which I started more than twenty years ago, the attempt to write a parallel history of Greek art and literature from Homer to Menander. I cannot say now what gave me the original impulse but I can still remember various events which contributed to it when I was an undergraduate—Sir John Beazley's lectures on Greek vase-painting, Sir John Myres's equation of Homeric composition with Geometric art, a cursory reading of Spengler's *Untergang des Abendlandes*, and curiously enough a hearing of Reger's orchestral suite on three pictures of Boeckhlin. An early interest in Sophocles led me to consider the fifth century first, and *Greek Art and Literature, 530-400 B.C.* (O.U.P.) was published in 1939. During the war I gradually collected material on Menander, who had interested me from the time when I worked under Alfred Koerte at Leipzig after going down from Oxford, and from this starting point I made the survey published as *Art and Literature in fourth century Athens* (Athlone Press) in 1956. In 1952 Michael Ventris discovered that the Linear B script was used for recording Greek, and from his article with John Chadwick in the *Journal of Hellenic Studies* for 1953 it became clear that Mycenaean art was Greek art and that conclusions could now be drawn as to the nature of Mycenaean poetry: this I tried to show in *From Mycenae to Homer* (Methuen, 1958), which was a first attempt to study the development of Greek art and literature from the time of the Mycenaean shaft graves to the time of the *Iliad* and *Odyssey*.

The de Carle lectures are designed to fill the gap between Homer (and I mean by Homer the *Iliad* and the *Odyssey*) and the beginning of my first book, the period of some two hundred years which covers the early elegiac and lyric poets, the beginnings of Greek sculpture, and black-figure vase-painting. But I must also explain the subtitle, the beginnings of modern civilization. I still believe that a parallel history of art and literature has value for itself, but I have since the war become increasingly interested in studying the history of Greek civilization as the history of a people who stepped right out of their context and developed entirely new ways of thinking and seeing, much as Western Europe did after the Renaissance, drawing heavily on Greek ideas and so laying the foundations of our modern world civilization.

In what respects however can we say that the ancient Greeks were modern, more modern than the Middle Ages, more modern than large portions of humanity today? Many elements in human life are universal and these do not interest us except in so far as they may give us evidence for something else: thus at all times and in all places men have made love, fought, played games, told stories, delighted in some kind of music, and had some sort of respect for whatever governed events beyond human control. Other elements in our present civilization are recent applications of pure science to practical ends—printing, railways, aeroplanes, telephones, television, space travel and the like. It is possible that these developments are so revolutionary that they constitute a third leap out of context, parallel to the Greek leap and to the Renaissance leap. Certainly they are important enough, if we believe that history has any lessons at all, to justify careful study of the technique and conditions of the preceding leaps. That is much more than I can attempt in these lectures. The most I can do is to sketch the beginning in the seventh and sixth centuries B.C. of three essential elements in modern civilization: individual responsibility, drama, science and philosophy.

I must however first explain how these things seem to me to fit together as essentials of ancient Greek and of our modern civilization. I hope we should all agree that, whatever the demands of the state, the state only exists to ensure as much freedom to the individual as is compatible with the freedom of the other individuals forming the state, and that, although individuals are unequally gifted by nature and therefore of necessity unequally rewarded, they are equal as morally responsible for their actions. The political story of the gradual achievement of full democracy in ancient Greece has often been told, and I shall only allude to it in passing: I may remind you here that in Athens the laws of murder and homicide were inscribed in a public place for the first time in the seventh century, that at the beginning of the sixth century Solon secured for all citizens the essential rights of voting in the Assembly and sitting on juries, that Athens like many other Greek cities was governed unconstitutionally by a single citizen for a period in the sixth century (what the Greeks called 'tyranny'), but that by the end of that century democracy was firmly established and full democracy in sight. But I shall consider more fully what the poets and artists tell us about themselves, what sort of detail they include in their portraits of others, what kind of responsibility they demand in their fellows.

I do not think that it is fanciful to suppose that drama was a new kind of literature invented to meet this new interest in individual responsibility. Of course, in this crude form such a statement is obviously untrue, and drama has a long and complicated ancestry which we shall have to discuss. It is true, however, that the official beginnings of Greek tragedy lie late in our period, that the responsibility of the individual is the central problem of Aeschylean drama and that for the two centuries through which we can follow the history of Greek drama the development is towards more and more detailed portraits of individuals reacting to their fellows. Essentially tragedy is a new method of presenting the old heroic stories by which the heroes of the past appear as men of today acting and speaking in relation to each other.

From this same insistence on the value of the individual we can, I think, also derive the beginnings of philosophy and science. The view of the universe which the philosophers and scientists provide is a new view of the universe. Its newness is threefold: it is based on observations which anyone can check, it is seen in terms of models which are intelligible to everyone, it is justified by arguments which everyone can understand. The rational explanations of the scientist differ completely from the vision of the prophet, and perhaps the essential difference is that the scientist is not a seer but a teacher and the corollary of this is that his audience are not blind receivers but responsible individuals, potentially as clear-sighted as himself. In one respect the work of the scientist has an analogy with the work of the dramatic poet and the work of the realistic painter and sculptor. Each of them is concerned with stating accurately what can be observed and with drawing certain conclusions from the observations; they differ, of course, in that the scientist states the conclusions, whereas the dramatist and painter leave them to his audience to draw. What however is common to all three and what is new is that the observations are presented directly without interpretation to the audience. The scientist records his observations before interpreting them, the dramatist can only speak through the words and actions of his characters, the painter can only suggest the underlying whole through the shapes which are actually visible. Thus we shall find that not only science and drama but also three-dimensional painting and sculpture begin in this period.

But before discussing these questions in detail some general idea must be given of the characters about whom I shall be speaking. They must be shown against their background and in their setting.

I

The Characters in Their Setting

MICHAEL VENTRIS'S discovery that Linear B was used for recording Greek has thrown a flood of light on the Greek world in the second millennium[1]. Many of the details are obscure but it is at least clear that Homer preserved the memory of a complex Greek civilization which flourished upwards of five hundred years before the date of our *Iliad* and *Odyssey*, and that the Greek gods and heroes were in the main already established at that time. When I call the civilization of the second millennium complex, I mean that it consisted of a number of palaces, of which Knossos, Mycenae, and Pylos are the best known, each ruled by a King who was treated as divine and had the goddess who protected him living with him in his palace. The palaces were linked together in some sort of feudal system under the great King of Mycenae, and were in contact with the civilizations of the East, Egypt, Babylon, Troy, the Hittites, the various Semitic kingdoms on the Syrian coast, and, perhaps most important of all, the older Minoan civilization of Crete, which seems to have been itself Asiatic in origin. Mycenaean settlements were founded on the coast of Asia Minor and Syria. Warriors, poets, and artists voyaged from court to court within and without the Mycenaean world and their commerce consisted of stories, ideas, and art forms; so that already in the second millennium Greek poetry absorbed some of the great Eastern stories, the Gilgamesh epic, the Creation Myth, and Keret's siege of Udum, and Greek poets retold them of their own gods and heroes. Nothing could be less modern (in the sense defined above) than the picture which can now be drawn of the divine Mycenaean King 'tippling like an immortal' out of his golden cup as he sat on his throne flanked by griffins and lionesses, which symbolized divine protection and his own power. But he left to his successors a fund of great stories, a memory of a rich civilization in Greece, a memory of the East as a good place for settlement and a source of riches not only material, and finally, I think we must add, a respect for craftsmanship in poetry and art.

The great Mycenaean palaces were destroyed in the thirteenth and twelfth centuries, and most of Central and Southern Greece was occupied by invaders from the North, who were akin to the Mycenaeans in language but had not been civilized by contact with older civilizations. Athens alone survived, and Athens became the rallying point for refugees; from Athens a stream of refugees with memories of earlier Mycenaean settlements founded the new cities on the coast of Asia Minor between roughly 1035 and 900, but it seems unlikely that there was much fruitful contact with the East before 800 [2]. In this long period of poverty and isolation the old stories were told and retold by oral poets, and however many anachronisms were introduced Mycenaean memories were kept alive. Much that happened escapes our notice, but one political change and one artistic change are of great importance. The divine King went with his palace; even in Athens, where the Acropolis was not captured, the archaeologists have found evidence that the Royal palace became the house of the goddess Athena very soon after the Mycenaean period, and that the King, who was now called by the humbler title of *basileus* instead of the Mycenaean title of *wanax*, lived elsewhere. The *basileus* was drawn from a particular family, but evidently other members of the family also claimed their rights, and in due course other families demanded their share of privileges. Thus the long journey to democracy was begun [3].

The second change is the change in the decoration of Athenian pottery, which rapidly spreads to the rest of the Greek world [4]. As pottery was always a major art among the Greeks we are justified in seeking a corresponding general change of spirit. The figure scenes, animal life, and plant life which enlivened Mycenaean pottery were abandoned for simple geometric ornaments executed with mathematical precision and love. Very occasionally horses were depicted on the vases which we call protogeometric, and figure scenes were reintroduced on geometric vases before the middle of the eighth century: but animals and men were subjected to the same precise abstraction. Tentatively I should like to suggest that the spirit behind this new art is a belief in human reason, in human capacity to reduce things to simple and clear patterns so that they become manageable. Certainly this love of clear and precise pattern survived in Greek art as a basis of composition, feebly it is true in the seventh century but much more strongly again in the sixth, more weakly always in the softer landscape of Greek Asia Minor and the Islands than amid the hard outlines of Attica and the Peloponnese; but in Greek Asia Minor it found another expression in early physics and mathematics. I see the same basic spirit again in the unromantic unmysterious view of the gods as differing from man only in strength and durability[5]. This view excluded the ecstatic and magic elements in Mycenaean religion, and we shall find that they re-emerged in the seventh century only to be reduced again to system in the sixth.

In the eighth century poverty and isolation belonged to the past. The Greek cities in Asia Minor were well established and had their own trading post at Al Mina at the mouth of the Orontes, through which stories as well as works of art would be exported to the West, and from the middle of the century contact with the East is manifest in many ways[6]. On the Greek mainland Athens was producing her superb late geometric pottery, and the first Greek colonies in Italy were founded just before the middle of the century. The dominant figure of the middle of this century was Homer, and by Homer I mean the author or authors of the *Iliad* and the *Odyssey*. As I see it, Homer was a genius who exploited three existing conditions, love of the past, love of festivals, and the alphabet[7]. None of these was quite new when Homer wrote. It was natural enough that the cities which had Mycenaean origins should preserve Mycenaean memories through the dark period, but in the eighth century the new city of Corinth claimed the Mycenaean hero Bellerophon as a Corinthian, the Dorian aristocracy of Sikyon had choruses singing of the sufferings of the Mycenaean hero Adrastos, and somebody in Boeotian Thebes forged an inscription so as to be able to display a tripod as a dedication by Amphitryon, the father of Herakles[8]. Eighth century wealth made festivals possible on a greater scale than before[9], and it was for festivals that Homer composed his epics—the *Iliad*, as I think, for the Panionian festival of Poseidon on the promontory between Ephesos and Miletos, and the *Odyssey* for the festival of Apollo at Delos.

The invention of the alphabet, which was borrowed and adapted from the Phoenicians at most a hundred years before the composition of the *Iliad*[10], made possible the recording of a long epic so that it could be recited by relays of reciters. It is very likely that narrative epics in chronological order had been recited at the great festivals for half a century before the *Iliad* was written. Homer's narrative is not straightforward: it is an extremely complicated and involved composition (for which the only parallel is contemporary Attic vases) and its balances and rhythms, preparations and back references can only be appreciated when heard in continuous recital. Thus he was the first poet and, if he also wrote the *Odyssey*, the last poet to exploit the new conditions to the full. The *Iliad* and the *Odyssey* might be called the Death and Transfiguration of the Greek oral epic.

Homer looks both backwards and forwards. He is in the direct line of descent from the court poets of Mycenaean Pylos. His idiom is still the idiom of Mycenaean court poetry, which had become the convenient mnemonic of post-Mycenaean oral poets but which for him again was a live style expressing a particular view of life in which the essential and typical was more important than the transitory and particular[11]. This style could not survive the birth of individualism any more than its parallel in art, the figure style of geometric painting; and the ease of alphabetic writing and reading destroyed its mnemonic convenience. The audience of the *Iliad* and *Odyssey* was no longer the court or even the big house but the great festival attended by the well-to-do citizens of many cities, and in many passages Homer takes them into account. They were the hoplites who formed the fighting line of their cities, and here and there the traditional Mycenaean battles are related as if they were modern hoplite battles. They were individuals, and among the late passages in Homer in which eighth century language is clearest are those in which the difficulties of individual decision are stressed and a new terminology is developed for describing mental characteristics[12].

The *Odyssey* and probably also the *Iliad* (though it was originally composed for the festival at Mykale) were performed every four years at the festival of Apollo at Delos until late in our period when the performance was transferred to the great festival of Athena at Athens[13]. Delos is a convenient place from which to survey the characters of our period. It is a tiny rocky island in an incredibly blue sea in the middle of the chain of islands which stretches across from the mainland of Greece to the coast of Asia Minor. The god Apollo and the goddess Artemis were born there, and the island was regarded as a holy place continuously from Mycenaean times[14]. We have an account of a festival of Apollo in the hexameter hymn to Apollo, which the Greeks ascribed to Homer himself. The poet describes first how the other gods were frightened when the archer god appeared among them, then how his mother Leto with difficulty persuaded the island Delos to receive her when she gave birth to Apollo. Apollo states his wish (131): 'May my love be the lyre and the curving bow. And I will proclaim to men the true will of Zeus.' Then the poet goes on to describe the festival, and finally ends with Apollo's arrangements for founding his other great sanctuary, the oracle at Delphi[15].

Not long after the composition of the hymn, perhaps still in the seventh century, the sculptors Tektaios and Angelion made a new 9ft. image for Apollo's new temple[16]. They made it of wood and plated it with gold. The god was naked except for a belt and had a bow in his left hand and little statues of the three Graces in his right hand. The three Graces held one a lyre, the second a flute, and the third pipes; they can be imagined from a group of three Muses attending the wedding of Peleus on a sixth century Attic vase[17]. The Delian god was given Graces rather than Muses because they were also musical, they were a trio, and they were revered in Delos. So the double nature of the god was rendered by the sculptor: the bow shows that he deals out disease and death, the Graces that he is the patron of music and poetry. A work of the same school but rather earlier is a small limestone statue in Paris, which has been recognized as our nearest likeness to the Aphrodite of Delos described by Pausanias[18]: 'a small statue its right hand damaged by time; it goes down into a square block instead of feet.'

The description of the festival in the hymn to Apollo must be quoted in full (146):

In Delos, Apollo, dost thou most rejoice, where the long robed Ionians gather with their children and their ladies. They rejoice thee with boxing and dancing and singing when they hold a contest in memory of thee. He would think the Ionians were deathless and ageless who saw them when they were gathered. He would see the grace of them all, and his soul would rejoice at the sight of men and fair-girdled women and swift ships and their many possessions. There is also another marvel, the fame of which shall not perish, the maidens of Delos, servants of far-shooting Apollo, who, when they have sung first in memory of Apollo and then of Leto and archeress Artemis, sing a song of men and women of long ago and charm the tribes of men. They can imitate the speech and rhythm of all men, and each would think that he himself was speaking. So beautifully is their song composed.

But now may Apollo and Artemis bless us, and fare you all well. But remember me again in the future whenever a stranger comes here after many troubles and asks you: 'Maidens, who is the sweetest singer on the market here and in whom do you most rejoice?' Do you then all make answer about us: 'A blind man and he dwells in rocky Chios. His songs are much the best hereafter.' And we will bring your fame over the earth as far as we go among the well-inhabited cities of men.

This is a fascinating exposé of the economics of early Greek poetry. First, there is the contest, and it is a reasonable supposition that the poet composed the hymn to Apollo for a contest at Delos. This was presumably a contest for original poetry as distinct from the recitation of the *Iliad* and the *Odyssey*, in which the successive reciters (*rhapsodes*) competed in reciting from an established text. A later form of poetic contest was the dramatic contest at the festivals of Dionysos at Athens at which not only the tragic and comic poets but also the actors competed [19]. The Boeotian poet Hesiod tells us of another contest at the end of the eighth or the very beginning of the seventh century and we get another glimpse of how early Greek poetry was produced (*Op.* 650): 'I never yet sailed in a ship over the broad sea except to Euboea from Aulis, where once the Achaeans waited for a storm when they had collected much people from holy Greece against Troy, land of fair women. From there I crossed to Chalkis for the funeral games of warlike Amphidamas. The sons of that great man had announced many prizes which they offered. There I say I won with a hymn and bore away a handled tripod, which I dedicated to the Muses of Helikon, where first they set me on the path of clear song.' This contest was held at the funeral celebrations of the King of Chalkis in Euboea, and the elaboration of the reference to the mustering of the Greek army at the beginning of the Trojan war has suggested that Hesiod's hymn described the course of events from the marriage of Helen to the Trojan War [20].

This kind of contest in epic recitation must have been one of the means by which the knowledge of Greek mythology was kept alive among the Greeks. I think we have to suppose that the rapid spread of writing over the Greek world in the eighth century [21] was followed by an equally rapid recording of the ancient stories which had been handed down by oral tradition and were now written down as hexameter poetry still largely composed in the old oral manner. Although only the *Iliad* and the *Odyssey* of Homer and the *Theogony* of Hesiod survive complete, we have fragments of other poems particularly on the Trojan War story and the names and dates of a number of poets [22]. These poems were presumably composed for particular festivals, but once they had been recited there they could be recited also elsewhere, wholesale or piecemeal, by the wandering reciter wherever he went 'among the well-inhabited cities of men'. The activity of the wandering reciters is reflected in the very large number of mythical scenes which appear in Greek art in the seventh century, and when we find before the middle of the seventh century vases made in Athens, Argos, and Italy illustrating Odysseus' adventures with the Cyclops [23], we can infer that recitations of the ninth book of the *Odyssey* were widely popular.

If we look a little wider and a little later in our period, we see far more evidence of the reflection of these recitations in art [24]. The excavations at Olympia have yielded a large number of small bronze reliefs with a wide range of mythological scenes, which were used as buckles to hold the hoplite shields in place on their wearers' arms [25]. They were made by Argive artists and cover the whole of the sixth century and rather more; they give direct testimony to the hoplite's interest in mythology. In most cases the artists seem to have been inspired by epic but very occasionally we can suggest a lyric source. The hoplites were the ordinary well-to-do citizens, and it was they also who originally bought the large number of black-figure vases with mythological scenes produced in Athens, Corinth, Sparta,

Chalkis, and elsewhere from the late seventh century down to the end of our period (many of them reached Etruria and other places overseas by the secondhand market) ²⁶. Sometimes we can prove that they were special orders because a name against one of the figures is written in a form which belongs neither to the source nor to the artist: thus an East Greek plate ²⁷ of about 600 found in Rhodes has *Menelas* inscribed against one of the figures in a scene from the seventeenth book of the *Iliad*: Homer calls him *Menelaos* and the East Greek artist would have written *Meneleos; Menelas* is Peloponnesian and must be due to a Peloponnesian purchaser who instructed the painter what to write. The vase paintings normally seem to be inspired by epic, but here again we can occasionally suggest a lyric source. The ordinary citizen too must have enjoyed the mythological scenes on the temple of Artemis at Corcyra, on the Sicyonian treasury at Delphi, or on the treasury at Foce da Sele near Paestum in Southern Italy, to name only three outstanding collections of sculptural relief produced in the first quarter of the sixth century ²⁸. In sculpture also the main inspiration seems to be epic. Therefore one result of these epic recitations was that the new poets, who abandoned the old manner and the old metre and sang instead of reciting, could assume their audiences to have knowledge of mythology in its traditional forms, much as until recently poets could assume knowledge of the Bible: the stories would be retold with new emphasis or for a new purpose, or could simply be used to point a contrast or an allusion ²⁹.

The blind man from rocky Chios who composed the hymn to Apollo was evidently such a wandering reciter, whether he was, as the ancients thought, Homer himself or an early member of the poets' guild on the island of Chios who called themselves Homeridai or 'sons of Homer'; but the Delian maidens, whom he asks to advertize him in return for his advertizing them were a choir, the mortal counterpart of the Muses who served Apollo on Olympos ³⁰. The hymn shows that there were other poetic occasions besides the contests of which we have spoken: a stranger might arrive 'after many troubles' and want to thank Apollo for saving him from his troubles. A suitable thankoffering would be a song sung by the Delian maidens, and then for this he might need a poet and the Delian maidens would refer him to the blind man who dwelt in rocky Chios.

But there were two other possibilities. One is not stated in the hymn because it involved neither the choir nor the Chian poet. The stranger might send his own choir to sing a song composed by a compatriot or near compatriot. Pausanias [31] tells us that in the late eighth century the Corinthian poet Eumelos, who claimed the Mycenaean hero Bellerophon as an early Corinthian and showed Corinthian interest in colonization by naming his muses after places in the Black Sea, wrote a poem in hexameters in Doric dialect for the people of Messenia to celebrate their victory over the Spartans, and that this poem was performed in honour of Apollo at Delos by a Messenian choir.

The third possibility was that the stranger who wanted to thank Apollo with a hymn might hear from the Chian poet (or from a recitation of his hymn by another) that the Delian maidens 'can imitate the speech and rhythm of all men', and therefore he might employ his own local poet, knowing that the Delian maidens, when asked to sing the hymn, would not be frightened by his dialect or his metre. More interesting to us than the adaptability of the choir is the need for the choir to be so adaptable. This is precious early evidence for dialect songs in local metres, precious early evidence for the individualism of local poets. Thus we have on the one hand the local varieties of sung poetry and on the other hand the internationalism of Epic-Ionic spoken poetry. The recited hexameter poetry of which we have spoken preserves the Homeric dialect, the dialect of the Ionian cities of Asia Minor with a slight admixture of Aeolic, partly new and partly old, from the more northerly cities of the Asia Minor coast and a large substratum of Mycenaean. The same language essentially was used by writers in other metres, who naturally used the Ionic dialect, Kallinos of Ephesos and Mimnermos of Kolophon for elegiacs, Archilochos of Paros for elegiacs, iambics, and trochaics, Hipponax of Ephesos for iambics, Anakreon of Teos for lyrics—in fact for all the short poems sung at the banquets of the well-to-do. Long hexameter poetry [32] composed in areas outside the sphere of Ionic dialect nevertheless shows very few local forms, and the same is true of the hortatory elegiacs which Solon of Athens and Tyrtaios of Sparta addressed to their fellow citizens. But the short elegiac poems preserved in inscriptions [33] (epitaphs, dedications and the like) always show the local dialect even when they preserve

Homeric phrases. It is unlikely that this contrast is due to our texts; I think we must assume a difference between elegiac poetry sung in company and elegiac poetry used on private and public monuments. When he sang his elegiacs, the poet felt that he was in epic-Ionic tradition, but the short poems for monuments were felt to belong to the local tradition and therefore preserved the local dialect adapted as necessary to the scansion (it should be remembered that Athens and Boeotia at least shared a common Mycenaean poetic heritage with the Ionians and that the divergence of dialect was comparatively recent).

The adaptability of the Delian maidens shows that on choral lyric Homeric epic exercised no such compulsion. Eumelos of Corinth wrote epic hexameters in Ionic-epic dialect, but the hexameters which he wrote for the Messenian choir to sing in Delos are in Corinthian dialect. Pure lyric metres whether for solo or chorus were always written in dialect. Let us ask what the Delian maidens might have been asked to sing and take the opportunity to say something of the centres in which lyric poetry was produced. Nothing from Athens or the Ionian cities on the islands or in Asia Minor would give them difficulty: we know, for instance, that Archilochos wrote choral lyric in honour of Dionysos and hymns to Demeter and Herakles [34], and we have a very little evidence (in addition to the pictures of choirs on vases [35]) for choral lyric in Athens [36]. Songs from the island of Lesbos would be quite different. We know most about Sappho and Alkaios, who lived at the end of the seventh and the beginning of the sixth century B.C. They wrote solo lyric in Lesbian vernacular in a distinctive group of metres, but they also wrote choral lyric, including hymns [37]. Alkaios' hymn to Apollo told how the god was ordered by Zeus to give oracles at Delphi but went first to the Hyperboreans in the furthest North and gave them laws before establishing his oracle in Delphi. This version contradicts the version of the foundation of the Delphic oracle in the Homeric hymn, which says nothing of the Hyperboreans; and a picture on a seventh century Cycladic vase [38] shows Apollo arriving in Delos with the two Hyperborean maidens, whose tombs were recognized in two Mycenaean tombs on the island. Alkaios evidently set out to honour Delphi at the expense of Delos (Alkaios' hymn to Hephaistos will concern us again later).

Two earlier choral poets who began their lives in Lesbos must be mentioned although nothing is left of their works. Terpander, the inventor of the seven-stringed lyre[39], won a victory at Sparta about 675 B.C., and Spartan choral lyric owed much to his continued residence there. Seventh century Sparta was not the grim military state which we know so well in the classical period. Towards the end of the century Alkman[40], probably himself a Greek from Sardis in Lydia, has left us a curious and difficult song sung by a chorus of maidens in predominantly trochaic metre and Spartan dialect (1 D). They tell at length an obscure myth of how Herakles killed the sons of Hippokoon and draw the moral that mortal endeavour must be limited: they then describe the rivalry of choruses in the service of the Spartan goddess Ortheia, a fertility goddess of terrifying aspect also worshipped with dances in which the priestess wore the mask of the goddess and the chorus the masks of ugly women.

Arion of Lesbos was at the court of the tyrant Periander of Corinth before the end of the seventh century and from there made a concert tour of Sicily and Southern Italy. At Corinth he invented something called 'the tragic manner' and wrote choral songs on mythical themes in honour of Dionysos, which were sung by men dressed as satyrs: these were the padded dancers who appear on many Corinthian vases, and one of their themes was certainly the return of Hephaistos[41]. Like Terpander, it seems probable that Arion dropped his native Lesbian and adopted the local Doric dialect for his choral lyrics[42]; the excellence of his lyrics and of those of his successors was probably the chief reason for the curious phenomenon that the choruses of Attic tragedy have at least a superficial Doric colouring whereas the dialogue is in good Attic. It is likely that the large number of mythological scenes which appear on Corinthian vases of the late seventh and early sixth century owe something to Arion. But, as I have noted already, it is difficult to distinguish pictures based on lyric from pictures based on epic. Where, however, a minor character is given a name which will not scan in hexameters, a lyric source may be supposed. On this evidence in Arion's time the Corinthians sang narratives of the sack of Troy, of the lamentation of Achilles by the Nereids (this had also reached Attica by 570), and of Dionysos and his satyrs[43]. Other themes of choral lyric in the Peloponnese during our period were the sufferings of Adrastos at Sikyon, and in Argos (or at least known to Argives) Herakles' descent to Hades and Ajax' rescue of the body of Aristodemos (a local hero of whom we know nothing)⁴⁴.

When we find, at the same date and a little later, a first rate lyric poet in Sicily who writes choral lyric on a wide range of mythological themes in a dialect touched with Dorian, it is natural to suspect that the art of this local poet Stesichoros had been fostered by the great Lesbian poet Arion when he visited the West⁴⁵. For Stesichoros we have a string of titles and scanty fragments: a new papyrus gives fragments of eighteen lines, in which Helen and Menelaos say farewell to Telemachos when he starts on his way back to Ithaca. Stesichoros made some changes as well as condensing the narrative of the *Odyssey*, but it is difficult to·see significance or great poetry here. However the Helen poem in which Stesichoros stated that she had never gone to Troy seems to have been an original version, and in his *Oresteia* he shifted the scene of the story from Mycenae to Sparta, introduced Orestes' nurse, made Klytaimnestra dream of a snake, and gave Orestes a bow to ward off the Furies. On the metopes at Foce da Sele Klytaimnestra is forcibly restrained from attacking Orestes with an axe and the excavators have suggested that the woman holding her back is Orestes' nurse and the source Stesichoros.

How much this Western poetry was known in Greece itself is a matter for debate, but another poet will guide us back to the Greek cities of Asia Minor and their art and philosophy. Ibykos of Rhegium in S. Italy may well have known Stesichoros, and his mythological poems may well have followed the same lines as the earlier poet⁴⁶. But soon after the middle of the century he migrated to the court of the tyrant Polykrates of Samos and there was celebrated for his love poetry (8 D): 'Euryalos, scion of the blue-eyed Graces, darling of the fair-tressed Muses, Aphrodite and soft-lidded Persuasion reared you among roses.' If we want to imagine Euryalos, we can look at the long-haired, soft, well-covered boy holding two horses on the Otago hydria, which was painted by an Ionian artist towards the very end of our period; and 'soft-lidded Persuasion' can be illustrated by the earlier almond-eyed beauty from Ephesos in the British Museum⁴⁷.

If we add to this head a rather earlier body dedicated to the goddess Hera in Samos [48], we can form some idea of how an Ionian thought of his lady and learn that the artist was not behind the poet in the expression of sensuous beauty. Note the gaiety of colouring in the vase, the feeling for the different quality in the hair, eyes, cheeks and lips of the head, the differentiation of smooth veil, fine linen skirt, and heavier woollen mantle on the body. Sensuous beauty these works certainly have, but they also show intelligent and accurate observation, which is one of the roots of Ionian philosophy. The head comes from the great sixth century temple of Artemis at Ephesos, the body from the great sixth century sanctuary of Hera at Samos. A third great Ionian shrine was the temple of Apollo at Branchidae outside Miletos, from which a series of sixth century marble statues survives, substantial, richly draped men, seated on thrones, with inscriptions not in verse but in good workaday prose [49].

Miletos was the home of the three first scientists and philosophers, Thales, Anaximander, and Anaximenes, whose lives ran from soon after the middle of the seventh century to the end of our period. The Thales who dedicated a magnificent marble lion in Miletos cannot be our Thales, and the Anaximander who dedicated the statue of a girl about 560 may not have been the philosopher; but they were contemporaries, and these rich dedications give some idea of the milieu in which the philosophers lived. Though we shall be chiefly interested in their speculation, they were also practical men well rooted in this commercial civilization: they would do such useful things as foretelling an eclipse, or making a corner in olives; they invented the map and the sundial. Thales, as we shall see, was a considerable mathematician; Anaximander said that the orbit of the sun was twenty-seven times the earth's diameter and that the cylindrical earth's diameter was three times its depth [50]. Here the Greek desire for geometrical simplicity asserted itself once more, the desire to make the world rational and therefore controllable, a desire which first expressed itself in the decoration of Athenian pottery during the dark period after the fall of Mycenae and found its most extreme expression in the mathematical philosopher Pythagoras, who left Samos for the West about 530. Thus our period ends with a new rich style in literature and art, characterized by acute observation of sensuous detail within a framework imposed by a controlling sense of form[51].

Nearly two centuries earlier the blind poet from Chios spoke of the grace of the Ionians when they were assembled at Delos, of the marvellous aspect of 'men and fair-girdled women and swift ships and their many possessions'. Already at that date they were wealthy and the festival was an occasion for a fair, but that was only the beginning of their prosperity after the long struggle of settlement. Alphabetic writing was now well established, and the recording of poetry in local dialects and metres to express the individualities of the poets and their companions became a magnificent possibility. The new poets broke loose from the scale and manner of Homeric epic, just as the artists broke loose from the scale and manner of the geometric style to start on the long journey towards realistic representation of the individual. At the end of our period and by the middle of the sixth century a new compromise had been achieved between formal pattern and realistic content, a compromise beautifully represented by the poetry of Anakreon and the art of the great Athenian black-figure painters. The seventh century however is a time of revolution against Homeric and geometric conventions. The slim and graceful deer on a Parian amphora of the mid-seventh century[52] still has something of geometric abstraction, and the shape has something of geometric precision and definition; but no geometric artist would have painted a single deer on such a scale and in so much detail.

For me the essence of the revolution is seen in the Athenian black-figure vases of the late seventh century with their grand flowing shape and their magnificent, striding, violent figures and animals and monsters. This is the spirit and the style of the long elegiac poem in which the Athenian Solon justifies the ways of Zeus to men (1,17 D): 'Zeus watches over the completion of all things. Suddenly just as the clouds in spring of a sudden are scattered by the wind, which, having stirred the depths of the billowing barren sea and devastated the fair fields over the wheat-bearing earth, reaches the lofty seat of the gods in heaven and puts brightness before our eyes again; the strong sun shines fair over the rich land and there is no longer any cloud to see: such is the vengeance of Zeus.' When our period opens the dark romantic violence of this spring storm is just apparent on the horizon; when it ends the sun is shining again with a radiance which anticipates something of the classical glory of Sophocles and Pheidias, but before that another stormy, romantic period intervened, the period of the Persian wars, Aeschylus and the sculptures of Olympia.

NOTES TO CHAPTER I

THE CHARACTERS IN THEIR SETTING

(References to works of art will be found under the appropriate numbers
in the List of Monuments at the end.)

1. Michael Ventris's discovery and its results are fully discussed in M.
   Ventris and J. Chadwick, *Documents in Mycenaean Greek*, Cambridge,
   1956. The summary that follows is based on my *From Mycenae to
   Homer* (=*M.H.*), Methuen, 1958, Chs. 1-4.
2. Cf. *M.H.* Ch. 5. On the revival of Eastern contacts, see T. J.
   Dunbabin, *The Greeks and their Eastern Neighbours*, Hellenic Society,
   Supplementary Paper, no. 8, 1957 (=Dunbabin (1957); P. Amandry,
   Syria, 35 (1958), 73 f.; *Études d'Archéologie Classique*, 1 (1955), 1.
3. On early kingship besides *M.H.*, Ch. 5 and Ch. 8, 1, see D. L. Page,
   Sappho and Alcaeus, Oxford, 1955 (=Page), 149 ff., on seventh
   century Lesbos; A. Andrewes, *The Greek Tyrants*, Hutchinson, 1956,
   9 ff.
4. Cf. *M.H.* Chs. 7 and 9. A fine example of Attic geometric pottery
   is illustrated in fig. 1, a pitcher dated 760/40 in the National Museum
   at Athens, cf. *M.H.* 197 f.
5. Cf. E. Ehnmark, *The idea of god in Homer*, Uppsala, 1935; P. Chantraine, *Entretiens Hardt*, I, 64 f.
6. Al Mina: L. Woolley, *The Forgotten Kingdom*, Penguin Books, 1953,
   172 ff.; Dunbabin (1957), 25 f.
7. Cf. *M.H.*, Ch. 8, 5.
8. Bellerophon: Dunbabin, *Studies Presented to David M. Robinson*, II
   (1953), 1164 f. Adrastos: Hdt. 5, 67. Amphitryon: Hdt. 5, 59.
9. The Panionion on Mykale was founded at the time of the Ionian
   migration. Cf. H. T. Wade-Gery, *The Poet of the Iliad*, 3 f. The festival
   at Delos is dated by the Homeric hymn to Apollo to the late eighth
   century but may be earlier. Records at Olympia go back to 776 B.C.
10. Dunbabin (1957), 60 gives the limits as 850 and 750; so also W. F.
    Albright in *The Aegean and the Near East*, (Essays presented to Hetty
    Goldman), New York, 1956, 162. R. M. Cook and G. Woodhead
    (*A.J.A.* forthcoming) have suggested Al Mina as the place where
    borrowing took place: the different Greek cities made their own widely
    different adaptations.
11. *M.H.*, 70 ff., 237 ff.; cf. Adam Parry, *T.A.P.A.*, 87 (1956), 1.
12. *M.H.*, 255 ff.
13. Ancient authorities ascribe the introduction of the *Iliad* and *Odyssey*
    at the Panathenaea to Solon, Peisistratos, and Hipparchos. The
    Panathenaic games were instituted in 566. It is tempting to connect
    the introduction of the Homeric epics with the purification of Delos
    by Peisistratos. Cf. Gilbert Murray, *Rise of the Greek Epic*, 191 ff.;
    H. W. Parke, *C.Q.* 40 (1946), 106.

14. A Mycenaean throne decorated with ivory was apparently still on view in the eighth century when it was buried in the foundation deposit of the new Artemision (H. Gallet and J. Tréheux, *B.C.H.* 71-2 (1947-8), 148). Two Mycenaean tombs were revered as the tombs of the Hyperborean maidens (Ch. Picard, *B.C.H.*, 48 (1924), 247 ff.)

15. The farewell to the Delian maidens (166 f.) sounds like an end and many scholars have believed that a Delian hymn has been joined to a later Pythian or Delphic hymn, and the final product has been ascribed to Kynaithos of Chios in the late sixth century (cf. H. T. Wade-Gery in *Greek Poetry and Life*, 1936, 56 f. and on the other side F. Dornsieff, *Kleine Schriften*, I, 429). None of the external evidence for dating the Pythian hymn (e.g. most recently G. Forrest, *B.C.H.* 80 (1956), 1) seems to me compelling. I am more impressed by the linguistic statistics, which suggest that the Pythian part is at least as early as the Delian part and the hymn as a whole earlier than the *Hymn to Demeter* and the *Theogony* (Cf. Allen and Halliday, *The Homeric Hymns*, xcvi ff. and my article in *Glotta*, 1959).
    The foundation legends of Delos and Delphi were, of course, different, and it may be that our hymn is really a unity made out of two early hymns. What concerns me here is only the acknowledged earliness of the Delian part. On the opening scene of the Delian hymn and its probably Oriental origin cf. J. Kroll, *S.I.F.C.*, 27-8 (1956), 181.

16. Cf. R. Pfeiffer, *Journal of the Warburg and Courtauld Institutes*, 15 (1952), 20 f., who quotes all the evidence and interprets it by a new poem of Kallimachos. (fr. 114 Pf.) Tektaios and Angelion were pupils of Dipoinos and Skyllis, the Cretan sculptors, who were said to be pupils of Daidalos and migrated to Sikyon; they are dated by Pliny in the very early sixth century. Cf. Rumpf quoted on no. 9.

17. The François vase, no. 46; cf. the Nysai attending the wedding on Sophilos' dinos, no. 45.

18. Pausanias 9, 40, 3; no. 9, fig. 5.

19. The tragic contest at the Great Dionysia started officially in 534 B.C. Cf. below Ch. III and A. W. Pickard-Cambridge, *Dramatic Festivals of Athens*, Oxford, 1953, 56 f.

20. I owe this suggestion to Dr. Peter Walcot's unpublished dissertation, *Hesiod and the Boeotian Epic*. On the date of Hesiod's *Works and Days* see Wade-Gery, *The Poet of the Iliad*, 1. The papyrus fragments of the *Catalogue* are now published by R. Merkelbach, Leipzig, 1956.

21. We now have eighth century inscriptions from Athens, Ithaca ,Perachora (probably Megarian at that date, cf. N. Hammond, *B.S.A.* 49 (1954), 93 f.), Thebes, Corinth, Ischia. References: Athens, Dipylon jug, N.M. 192, *Ath. Mitt.* 18, pl. 10; Ithaca, *B.S.A.* 43 (1948), 81, no. 490; Perachora spits, *Perachora*, I, 257, nos. 1 and 3; Thebes, Mantiklos Apollo, (no. 1); Corinth, skyphos, *A.J.A.* 37 (1933), 605; Ischia, G. Buchner and C. F. Russo, *Rendiconti Lincei*, 1955, 215. Cf. also my article in *Glotta*.

22. On Hesiod cf. n. 20 above. Fragments of all are given in Kinkel, *Epicorum Graecorum Fragmenta*, 1877. The Oxford text of Homer gives

fragments of the so-called Cycle, the poems ascribed to Homer. Of the East Greek poets Arktinos of Miletos (*Ilioupersis*, *Aithiopis*), Stasinos (*Cypria*), Kreophylos of Samos (*Oechalia*, possibly including more of the Herakles story), and Lesches of Mitylene (*Little Iliad*) probably all wrote in the eighth century, well after the *Iliad* and the *Odyssey* (Cf. *M.H.*, 274), and Aristeas of Prokonnesos seems to have written his *Arimaspeia* in the seventh century (Cf. most recently C. M. Bowra, *C.Q.* 49 (1956), 1 f.). On the mainland Eumelos of Corinth is dated in the eighth century by his hymn for the Messenians (fr. 13 Kinkel). Dunbabin (*J.H.S.* 68 (1948), 65 f. cf. also *op. cit.* above n.8) shows how he introduced Medea (fr. 12) and Bellerophon into Corinthian pre-history and gave the Muses Black Sea names at the time of Black Sea colonization (fr. 17). He also wrote of Dionysos and Lycurgus (fr. 10). He may also have written on the Perseus story (Gialouris, *B.C.H.* 77 (1957), 293). Cf. also M. Untersteiner, *Antiquitas*, 6 (1951).

23. Attic: nos. 33, 37. Argive: no. 66, fig. 3. West Greek: no. 102.

24. A general account of recent work on archaic representation of myth is given in *Lustrum* 1 (1956), 94-7. Since then note F. Brommer, *Vasenlisten zur griechischen Heldensage*, Marburg, 1956; D. von Bothmer, *Amazons in Greek Art*, Oxford, 1957. Dunbabin (1957), 80 f. lists 'illustrations of epic and other stories in Greek art before the sixth century': here therefore I merely note the places from which the artists came, adding a few more examples (noting where they are later than the seventh century) and a few differently interpreted. I. *Trojan scenes. Kypria.* Spartan, Corinthian, Attic, Argive, Boeotian. Add wedding of Helen, Corinthian, 600/575 no. 73; Trojan Embassy, about 560, no. 84; Assembly of Trojans, Attic, no. 36. *Iliad.* Boeotian, Cycladic, East Greek, Spartan, Corinthian. Add Attic 'games of Patroklos' by Sophilos, about 570, no. 44. *Aithiopis.* Argive, Cycladic, Corinthian, Ionian, West Greek. Add Achilles and Penthesileia, Attic relief, about 600, no. 4. *Little Iliad.* Corinthian, Spartan, Boeotian, Cycladic. *Iliou Persis.* Boeotian, Argive. *Odyssey.* Attic, Argive, Etruscan. Add Ares and Aphrodite, Naxian, about 650, no. 90.
II. *Thebais.* Corinthian. Add Tydeus and Ismene, Corinthian, 575-50, *N.C.*, no. 1437 (the story was told by Mimnermos).
III. *Herakles.* Attic, Argive, Corinthian, Boeotian, Spartan. Add Herakles and Prometheus, Attic, no. 42; perhaps Lichas and Iole (rather than death of Aigisthos), Attic, no. 35; perhaps Lichas and the poisoned robe, Attic, no. 30. The sons of Eurytos, Corinthian, no. 69, have the same names as in Hesiod, fr. 130.
IV. *Theseus.* Corinthian, Argive, West Greek.
V. *Perseus.* Attic, Boeotian, Corinthian, Spartan, Argive (Cf. above n. 22 on Eumelos). Andromeda, Corinthian, 575/50, no. 80.
VI. *Bellerophon.* Corinthian, Attic. (Cf. above n. 22 on Eumelos, but one of the seventh century Attic Chimairas, no. 39, corresponds to the description in *Iliad* 6 and not to the Corinthian type).
VII. *Other Stories. Europa.* Boeotian, Argive. *Chelidon and Itys.* Corinthian. *Argonaut story.* Dunbabin quotes a doubtful Medea and

Jason on a Corinthian clay relief (cf. Eumelos, n. 22 above). Add Mopsos (?) wrestling, Attic, no. 38; Harpies, Attic no. 41; ?Orpheus, Corinthian, no. 65; ?Jason and snake, Corinthian, no. 68; funeral games of Pelias, 575-50, no. 83. *Birth of Athena*. Argive. *Zeus and Centaur*. Corinthian, no. 64. This probably should be interpreted as Zeus and Typhon; Typhon does not appear in the new standard form of a winged, snaky monster before the second quarter of the sixth century (Argive). Add *Adrastos* stopping the quarrel between Amphiaraos and Lykourgos, Argive, 575-50, no. 15. (Note that this is nearly contemporary with Kleisthenes, who stopped the Sikyonian choruses recounting the sufferings of Adrastos). *Return of Hephaistos*, see ch. III, n. 20.

25. Published by E. Kunze, *Olympische Forschungen* II, Berlin, 1950. The majority of the objects labelled Argive in the preceding note are 'shield-bands'.

26. *Attic black-figure vases:* for subjects see mythological index of J. D. Beazley, *Attic Black-figure Vase-painters*, Oxford, 1956 (=*A.B.V.*), and themes from myth and legend in index of J. D. Beazley, *Development of Attic Black-figure*, Berkeley, 1951 (=*D.B.F.*). *Corinthian black-figure vases:* Payne, *Necrocorinthia* (=*NC.*), with additions by R. A. Hopper, *B.S.A.* 44 (1949), 162, and on the earliest painters M. Robertson and T. J. Dunbabin, *B.S.A.* 48 (1953), 172. *Chalcidian vases:* A. Rumpf, *Chalkidische Vasen*, Berlin, 1927; in *Malerei und Zeichnung* (=Rumpf), 55, he states that recent finds in Euboea establish the place of origin as Chalkis and that therefore the vases were not made in Italy, as some have thought. *Laconian* (=*Spartan*) *vases:* A. Lane, *B.S.A.*, 34 (1934), 99; B. Shefton, *B.S.A.*, 49 (1954), 299; P. Pelagatti, *Annuario*, 33-4 (1955-6), 1 ff. *East Greek, Wild goat styles:* A. Rumpf, *J.d.I.*, 48 (1933), 55. *Chiot:* R. M. Cook, *B.S.A.*, 44 (1949), 158; J. Boardman, *B.S.A.*, 51 (1956), 55. *Fikellura:* R. M. Cook, *B.S.A.*, 34 (1934), 1. *Clazomenian etc.:* R. M. Cook, *B.S.A.*, 47 (1952), 123. *Caeretan:* J. K. Anderson, *J.H.S.*, 75 (1955), 1; J. M. Hemelrijk, *de Caeretaanse Hydriae*, 1957. The artist (or artists) was certainly an Ionian, even if he worked in Etruria.

Some instances of the very large range of mythological scenes on sixth century vases have been already noticed, and more are mentioned below. The mythological themes listed in the index of *D.B.F.* amount to more than 75. The François vase, Attic, about 570, no. 46, is a kind of mythical anthology and is decorated with the Marriage of Peleus and Thetis, the hunt of the Calydonian boar, Troilos at the fountain, the return of Hephaistos, Theseus' triumph, the chariot-race at Patroklos' funeral games, and the battle of Lapiths and Centaurs. Of Eastern Greek black-figure vases the Caeretan hydriae are remarkable for their literary subjects: e.g. no. 99 Arimaspian and griffin (from Aristeas of Prokonnesos); no. 96, Apollo and the infant Hermes (Homeric hymn); no. 100, Embassy to Achilles with the name Odios (Ajax' herald) inscribed (*Iliad* 9).

27. Euphorbos plate from a tomb in Kameiros, Rhodes, no. 92. Cf.
Menelas on the seventh-century Attic stand from Aegina, no. 34; the
Aeginetan evidently ordered it in Athens and took it home with him.
An Aeginetan purchaser also was responsible for *Athanaia* on the
Corinthian Chigi jug, no. 67, which then found its way to Etruria by
the secondhand market (I think there is no other way to account for
the presence in Etruria of vases which can only have been painted for
a special occasion, e.g. the Pronomos vase celebrating a victory with
a satyr play, *G.T.P.*, no. A 9, and I suspect that the secondhand
market was the normal way for very fine vases to reach the West).

28. *Corcyra pediment:* no. 13. I believe the artist started with a local
Gorgonheaded Queen of Beasts, like Ortheia at Sparta (see below
n. 40) and the goddess on the East Greek plate, no. 93; then, being a
Corinthian, he thought of Perseus' Gorgon and added Pegasos and
Chrysaor. In the corners, he put the death of Priam and Zeus killing
a Titan.
Sicyonian treasury: no. 14. Metopes: Europa; Calydonian boar;
Argonauts (incl. Orpheus); cattle-raid; Bellerophon; Phrixos.
Foce da Sele: no. 29. A series of sandstone metopes: 1-17 Herakles
stories (note 7-9, Herakles saves Hera from the attentions of satyrs);
18-23 Trojan war (note 21, death of Patroklos); 24-26, Oresteia
(Klytaimnestra restrained by the nurse from attacking Orestes); 27,
Turtle hero; 28-9, Tityos; 30-31, Rape of Leucippids; 32-3, boiling of
Pelias; 34, Europa.

29. Retelling particularly in choral lyric and hymns, cf. below n. 37.
Mythical allusion: e.g. Sappho 28 D (=17 L-P) 'Hera, help (my
friends on their way) as the Atreidai after the Trojan war only left
Lesbos, when they had sacrificed to Hera, Zeus, and Dionysos,' cf.
Page, ch. VI and 129 f. Alkaios 73 D (=38 L-P) 'Drink because when
you are dead you will not see the light again: Sisyphos thought he
would escape death but he could not in the end.' Cf. also Page 273 f.;
some of the short poems may have been merely retellings from a
particular point of view. Cf. most recently H. Eisenberger, *Der
Mythos in der äolischen Lyrik*, Frankfurt, 1956.

30. They are called 'servants of Apollo'; this means perhaps not only
that they were maintained by the temple but also that they were trained
by the temple since Apollo was the god of music. Cf. the woodworker
who is the 'slave of Athena', Hesiod, *Op.* 430.

31. References are given above, n.22.

32. e.g. Hesiod of Boeotia, Eumelos of Corinth, Lesches of Mitylene.

33. e.g. the early Attic inscription on the Dipylon jug (above n.21) gives
the a-stem genitive plural in the Attic form—*on*, but the texts of Solon
give the Ionic form—*eon* even where it has to be scanned as a mono-
syllable. The Boeotian Mantiklos inscription (above n.21) gives a
Homeric echo in Boeotian form with digamma but texts of Hesiod
always omit the digamma (on this cf. A. Hoekstra, *Mnemosyne*, 10
(1957), 222). Corinthian and Corcyran metrical inscriptions have

Doric vowels and consonants, and digamma is written where metrically desirable; but Eumelos' epic fragments are in Epic-Ionic.

34. Archilochos: Dionysos, 77 D (cf. below, p. 31); Demeter, 119 D; Herakles, 120 D.

35. Dramatic or rather pre-dramatic choruses (i.e. padded dancers, nymphs, knights, giants etc.) are noted in Ch. III. The François vase, no. 46, shows muses celebrating the wedding of Peleus and Thetis and a mixed dance of the boys and girls saved by Theseus; another vase by Kleitias, no. 47, shows a dance of Nereids. All these mythical choruses will have had counterparts in ordinary life. A female chorus, probably in honour of Demeter at the Thesmophoria, appears on a contemporary cup, no. 49, (cf. the Corinthian sacrificial procession with music, no. 75); another shows men singing the hymn to welcome an athletic victor (Beazley, *D.B.F.*, 22; cf. also no. 58). The funeral was accompanied by choral lamentation (J. Boardman, *B.S.A.*, 50 (1955), 51 f.).

36. In the second quarter of the sixth century (a) two vases, nos. 50, 51, give an Amazon fighting with Herakles as Pantariste, (b) on a vase by Kleitias, no. 47, a Nereid is called Kymatothea. Neither of these names will scan in hexameters and the source must therefore be a poem in lyric metre.

37. On chronology see Page, 150 ff., 157 f., 225. On metres see Page, 318 f.; A. M. Dale, *C.Q.*, 44 (1951), 124 f. It is difficult to be certain what is choral and what is solo; for instance, Sappho's Aphrodite poem (1 D, 1 L-P) is *not* a choral hymn but a solo cast in hymn form. The Marriage Songs, however, including the Marriage of Hektor and Andromache (55 D, 44 L-P), were presumably sung by choirs (see Page, 72, 119 f.). The Adonis fragment (107 D, 140a L-P) is certainly choral (and perhaps a dialogue between maidens and a priestess representing Aphrodite): 'Fair Adonis is dead, Kythereia. What are we to do? Beat your breasts, maidens, and rend your garments.' Alkaios' longer narrative hymns were presumably sung by choirs, e.g. Apollo 1 D, 307 L-P; Hephaistos 9 D, 349 L-P (See below, p. 63). On choral lyric in general see C. M. Bowra, *Greek Lyric Poetry*, 1 ff. (= Bowra).

38. Cycladic vase: no. 89. Probably the same subject on the reverse of the contemporary Attic vase, no. 35. The tombs of the Hyperborean maidens: above n. 14.

39. A seven-stringed lyre on an early seventh-century vase found at Aeolian Smyrna (*J.H.S.* 71 (1951), 248).

40. On Alkman, Bowra 16 f.; D. L. Page, *Alcman: the Partheneion*, Oxford, 1951. On Ortheia see Page, *Alcman*, 71 f.; *G.T.P.*, 130; and below, p. 65. Masks: no. 18.

41. Hdt. 1, 23 and the Suda on Arion. Cf. Bowra, 82; A. W. Pickard-Cambridge, *Dithyramb etc.*, 19; *G.T.P.*, 99, 135, and below, p. 63.

42. A Corinthian vase of the early sixth century, no. 74, shows Apollo and the Muses, who are labelled *Moisai;* the Corinthian form to be expected is *Mousai* (Bechtel, *Gr. Dial.*, 2, 230) and *Moisai* is good Lesbian; but if Pausanias is to be trusted, Eumelos already used *Moisa* in the Messenian hymn (13 Kinkel).

43. Corinthian vases: Sack of Troy, no. 82, *Hipponika;* Nereids, no. 81, *Kumatotha = Kumatothea* (cf. *Penthesila = Penthesileia*) with other Nereid names unknown to Homer or Hesiod (Attic, cf. above n. 36b). Dionysos and his satyrs, no. 78; the names *Komios, Paichnios, Lordios, Loxios, Whadesios* belong not to the dancers themselves but to the 'satyrs' they represent. They probably occurred in a string (like Nereid names) and such a string would be trochaic.

44. Adrastos: cf. above n. 8, 24. Argive shield bands: Herakles' descent, no. 17: the hyperdoric form *Thaseus* suggests a lyric source. Ajax and Aristodemos, no. 16.

45. On Stesichoros see Bowra, 77 ff. The new papyrus: *Ox. Pap.* 2360. Helen: 11 D; Bowra, 120 f. Oresteia: 12-15 D, Bowra, 125 f. Bowra, 107, rates very highly the influence of Stesichoros on late seventh and early sixth-century Greek art and has made an extremely interesting case for this. That he influenced Western art is extremely likely, and the excavators of Foce da Sele have added new possibilities including the Oresteia metopes (nos. 24-26, cf. note 28 above). Kunze has also noted possibilities on the Argive shield-bands, including Herakles' descent into Hades (cf. n. 44 above). The first difficulty is the impossibility of distinguishing what lyric source the artist is using, even where (as noted above) we can say that he was using a lyric source. General coincidence of subject matter does not prove anything, and the difficulties raised by two important points of detail suggest caution. We are told that Stesichoros was the first to dress Herakles in lionskin, bow, and club (Athenaeus 512 f.) and that he was the first to make Athene leap in armour from the head of Zeus (Schol. Ap. Rhod. 4, 1310). Herakles appears so dressed on a Cycladic vase of the late seventh century, no. 91, and Athena is so represented on an Argive shield-band of the same date, no. 11. It is difficult to believe that Stesichoros (born 632-629) affected mainland and Cycladic art so early, and it may be safer to suppose that 'the first' means the first whose works have survived; my inclination is to suppose that Stesichoros owes more to earlier sources (including Arion) than we can now detect.

46. On Ibykos see Bowra, 248 f.; *G.A.L.* 7; Fränkel, *D.P.*, 366 f., *W.F.* 43 ff.

47. Otago Caeretan hydria, no. 98, fig. 15. Ephesos head, no. 25, fig. 6.

48. Statue dedicated by Cheramyes, no. 22.

49. A good discussion of the Hera sanctuary in Samos will be found in Karo, 39 f. The Branchidae statues are now in the British Museum, see F. N. Pryce, *Catalogue of Sculpture*, I, part 1. The lion (B 281) was dedicated in the early sixth century by Thales and other sons of

Orion (the inscription is in prose; cf. also the inscriptions of Chares, no. 26, at Miletos and of Aeakes at Samos, no. 27); the philosopher Thales was son of Examyes. Anaximander's kore: no. 23. Dedications by the sons of another Anaximander, son of Mandromachos, Pryce p. 105.

50. Texts are given by Diels-Kranz, *Fragmente der Vorsokratiker* (= *VS*): Thales A 1, 5, 10; Anaximander A 1, 10, 11. Cf. G. Kirk and J. Raven, *The Presocratic Philosophers*, Cambridge, 1957, 75 f.; 102 f.; 134 f. On Anaximander's proportions see also W. Jaeger, *Paideia*, I, 215; F. Lasserre, *Mus. Helv.*, 15 (1958), 13 f.

51. For a general description of sixth-century Ionia cf. my *Greek Interpretations*, 25 f. For the sensuous style and the sophisticated style in art and literature during the last half of the sixth century cf. *G.A.L.* 3-30.

52. Parian amphora: no. 88, fig. 2.

53. Particularly the work of the Nettos painter and his fellows: nos. 39-42. On Athens at this time in general and an interpretation of Solon's poem see *Greek Interpretations*, 13 ff.

II

The Individual and His Responsibility

IN the *Iliad* and *Odyssey* the great heroes stand out as individual figures, and Homer was particularly interested in them when they took difficult decisions or exhibited characteristics which were not contained in the traditional picture of the fighting man. These psychological passages of Homer are demonstrably late; they were added to the tradition by the last poet, who already saw the new hoplite society growing in the Ionian cities, a society based on all the fighting men of the cities not only on the leaders from the big houses [1]. But although Homer individualized the heroes of the past, he has told us nothing about himself or his contemporaries: his contemporaries appear in the similes but are never individualized; he himself only appears in his invocations to the Muses [2]: 'Tell me now Muses, who dwell on Olympos; for you are goddesses, you are present and know everything, but we only hear the report and know nothing—unless the Muses of Olympos, the daughters of aegis-bearing Zeus, remind me of all that came to Troy.' He does then make one claim for himself, that he has knowledge of the past, which the Muses have given him. This special knowledge he also attributes to the poets of the heroic age, like Demodokos in the *Odyssey*. In virtue of his claim to this knowledge, the poet probably had a rather special position even in Mycenaean times; the poet in whose care Agamemnon left Klytaimnestra when he went to Troy must have been something more than a court minstrel [3]. We may wonder how much authority they preserved during the dark years of the migrations when sterner skills must have been more in demand, but we can see how they not only restated their claims but also described their own individualities in the small and more stable hoplite societies of the seventh century.

In our period the poets not only described themselves but also other members of the societies in which they lived, and we shall have to consider how far they produced individual portraits, and whether the demands that they made on themselves and others were demands for individual responsibility. We shall then be able to set beside this series of literary portraits and self-portraits a series of portraits by artists, of which we can ask the same questions.

The author of the *Hymn to Apollo*, as we have seen [4], interrupted the story of Apollo's doings to tell us a little about himself and about the chorus in Delos: he describes the festival, the vocal skill of the Delian choir, and tells us that he himself is a blind man, a wandering singer who lives in rocky Chios and that his songs are extremely successful. We cannot say whether he was Homer or not, but it is clear that the hymn allows autobiography to an extent which would be improper in the large scale epic. He tells us a little about the choir and about himself, and when the choir sing they evidently are expected to mention him. It is interesting to see what becomes of this convention in the later choral poet Alkman, who wrote about the middle of the seventh century [5]. In the long papyrus fragment sung by a chorus of maidens he tells us of the beauty of Agido, who shines like a sun in the night festival, of the yet more beautiful leader of the chorus, Hagesichora, whose hair is like pure gold about her silver face, of golden bracelets, and Lydian headbands, of Nanno, Areta, Sylakis, Kleesisera, Astaphis, Philylla, Damareta, and Wianthemis, and of the trainer Ainesimbrota; he also gives some details of the actual performance. Many of the details are extremely difficult to interpret, but it is quite clear that Alkman describes the leader Hagesichora and her deputy Agido, and names the other members of the chorus (or more probably the members of a rival chorus). The audience wants to hear their names and what they are doing; this is an intimate affair and they are separate personalities. The beginning and the end of the song are lost so that we do not know whether the choir sang anything about the poet, but fragments of similar songs show that they sometimes did: (13 D) 'He was not a rustic nor unhandy nor among the unmusical nor a Thessalian by birth nor an Aetolian nor a shepherd, but from lofty Sardis'; (20 D) 'all our girls praise the lyre-player'; (49 D) 'and I will give you a tripod-cauldron in which to collect food of every kind. It has still not been touched by fire but soon it will be full of porridge, such as greedy Alkman loves hot after the solstice. For he does not eat elaborate dishes but seeks ordinary food, like the people' [6]. In this last fragment the chorus imagine someone else promising them a prize for their singing and the someone must almost be the judge of the contest. The tone is completely changed from that of the Homeric hymn; the small circle of girls, their audience, and the poet know each other and can joke with each other.

Hesiod is nearer both in time and spirit to the singer of the Homeric hymn to Apollo, and we have already noticed one of his autobiographical passages [7], in which he tells of his winning a tripod (the same prize as was to be given to Alkman's choir) for the performance of a 'hymn' at Chalcis. In the same passage he tells us how his father was a seafarer and abandoned Kyme in Aeolis for Askra in Boeotia, where Hesiod himself was born. He himself had only crossed the narrow strait from Aulis to Euboea: 'so little experience have I of bolted ships. But even so I will speak the mind of aegis-bearing Zeus. For the Muses have taught me to sing a marvellous song', and he then proceeds to discuss the right season for sailing. Like Homer he can appeal to the Muses for information outside his own experience. Unlike Homer, he has given us an account of his call to poetry [8]:

(The Muses) taught Hesiod a fair song long ago as he was pasturing his sheep beneath lovely Helikon. This word the goddesses spoke to me first, the Muses of Olympos, daughters of aegis-bearing Zeus: 'Shepherds of the fields, foul disgraces, mere bellies, we can tell many lies like the truth, we can tell the truth when we like.' So spoke the eloquent daughters of great Zeus, and granted me to pick a wondrous branch of blooming laurel as my staff and breathed into me divine speech that I might make known the past and the future.

It is useless to ask whether this is a real experience or not. The tradition of the god conversing with the king and giving him laws was very old, and the poetic theory of inspiration by the Muses was, as we have seen, Homeric. But this does not necessarily mean that Hesiod did not believe himself to have had this experience or that any Greek poet before had recounted such an experience to his audience. According to Hesiod the Muses established him as a reciter and *not* as a singer (that is the reason for the laurel branch); they established him as a poet and not as a shepherd only interested in food; they established him as a poet of truth and not only as a poet of lies. The distinction between truth and 'lies like the truth' must be a distinction between what we should call didactic

poetry and epic poetry. Hesiod, as we have seen, could and
did recite narrative epic about the heroes, but the particular
poem to which this is a prelude is a cosmogony followed
by a theogony: the origin of the world and the family tree
of the gods. These undoubtedly go back to Oriental sources,
and the outlines at least had probably entered Greek poetry in
Mycenaean times. But whatever his sources, the poem was for
Hesiod the truth and he guaranteed its truth by the account of
his consecration, which marked him off from ordinary men.

In virtue of this special relationship with the Muses he could
also preach the just life in the *Works and Days*—in the words of
the *Theogony* not only the past but also the future. Some of the
material here too is traditional, and the form (moral sermon
addressed to a member of the family) has Oriental parallels [9].
In form the poem is an appeal to his brother, Perses, to 'decide
the quarrel with a straight decision which comes from Zeus and
is therefore the best'; when the paternal property was divided
Perses had received more than his share because he bribed the
'Kings' who arbitrated between the brothers; now he has run
through his patrimony and demands more. In fact the poem is a
sermon to his audience: both the story of Pandora and the
story of the 'five ages' (gold, silver, bronze, heroic, iron) show
that we are living in a bad period, brutish, faithless, and unjust;
but Zeus will still reward justice and hard work, which in
practical terms means upright government by the nobles and
efficient and thrifty agriculture and seamanship for the rest [10].
We must suppose that Hesiod had a brother and was discon-
tented with the division of the property; but the appeal for a
new decision need have no legal reality; it is simply an occasion
for Hesiod's sermon, and the new decision itself would be
implemented if Perses took to hard work.

Hesiod and his brother were of course known in Askra and
the original arbitration was probably made by the nobles of
Thespiae, but his poetry soon passed outside Boeotia since it
was known to Archilochos in Paros by the middle of the seventh
century and to Alkaios in Lesbos by the end of the seventh
century [11]. We can only suppose that he recited at festivals in
Boeotia and perhaps across the border in Attica and central
Greece, and that other reciters took his poems overseas. He
stands out as an individual for two reasons: he tells us a good

deal about his life, and he has a message which he passionately believes: justice and hard work are rewarded by prosperity as surely as winter follows summer. This is the meaning of the new names, Good Order, Justice, and Peace, which he gives to the three seasons, the daughters of Zeus and Themis ('ordaining') [12]. Responsibility is placed on the individual, and the moral command is based on the physical workings of the universe. Thus Hesiod was himself an individual and appealed to men to accept their responsibility as individuals.

His consecration by the Muses was a model for many poets in the future. Other poets claimed miraculous experiences, like Arion, who was saved by a dolphin [13], but two early seventh-century poets had miraculous experiences directly connected with their poetry, Aristeas of Proconnesus, a city recently founded on an island in the sea of Marmara, and Archilochos of Paros. Aristeas [14] claimed that he was not bound by the ordinary rules of time and space. He could be snatched up by Apollo and put down among the Issedones, who lived North of the Caspian. He could die in Prokonnesos and reappear in Kyzikos. Thus it was possible in the fifth century for a South Italian Greek to maintain that he was Aristeas come to life again. Aristeas wrote a poem called the *Arimaspeia*, in which he told how Apollo had carried him into the land of the Issedones, and they had told him about the one-eyed Arimaspians, who lived beyond them and raided the gold guarded by the griffins. Aristeas presumably got his information from travellers' tales, and he belongs to the history of science in so far as he provides early evidence for Greek interest in non-Greek peoples, an interest which flowered later in Herodotos. From his informants he must also have heard of Shamans, whose souls could leave their bodies to associate with the spirits of the dead and return with wisdom to be communicated in poetry. He presented himself in his poem as a Greek shaman, carried off by Apollo to a distant land, and thus inaugurated a way of thinking about the soul as distinct from the body which involved, among other things, a quite new assessment of individuality. To this however we must return later.

About 680 the youthful Archilochos [15] was sent by his father from the harbour town of the island of Paros up into the mountains to fetch a cow to market; on his way down he met some women who asked him if the cow was for sale and said that they would give him a good price. Then the women and the cow vanished, and Archilochos found a lyre lying at his feet. He realized that the women were Muses and that he was destined to be a poet. It would be fascinating to know the truth behind this story, which Archilochos himself recounted in a poem[16]. He presumably felt that he, like Hesiod, should have a 'call' to poetry; possibly he had to account to his father for the loss of a cow and the acquisition of a lyre. Hesiod certainly expected others to believe in his 'call' and probably believed it himself. Archilochos, I suppose, neither believed nor expected complete belief, but it was a charming story for a young and brilliant poet to sing in the circle of his friends at Paros.

The poetry of Hesiod and Aristeas, in spite of the considerable autobiographic element and the contemporary subject matter, was still recited festival poetry in the metre and, to a large extent, the manner of Homeric epic. Archilochos' poetry was short poetry, sung to the accompaniment of lyre or flute to his friends in Paros. It shows none of the repetitive technique of oral poetry, which is still apparent in Hesiod, and was therefore composed in writing; from the beginning a text existed, and other poets recited it at festivals: it was certainly well known in Athens in the fifth century[17]. Presumably Archilochos sang at the drinking parties which followed dinner; how big his audience was we do not know. The number of people either addressed or named in his surviving poems amounts to about sixteen, and they were presumably the most famous or notorious men and women in the island, who were known to the majority of the hoplite class, the citizen soldiers of Paros. He wrote of their life and his own, of their struggles with the neighbouring Naxians, of the fortunes of the Parian colony in Thasos where he himself lived for a time, of a shipwreck in which his own brother-in-law and many other Parians lost their lives, of local elections, of prostitutes and profligates, of scandalous marriages, and of his own successes and disasters in love[18]. Very little of this is straight reporting or general encouragement to fighting men (like the elegiac poems of Kallinos of Ephesos or Tyrtaios of Sparta) or general political advice (like Hesiod's *Works and Days* or Solon's political poems) or general discourse on the pleasures of wine and making love (like much of Alkaios and

Mimnermos) [19]; nearly all Archilochos' poetry is written to or about particular persons on particular occasions.

Archilochos' account of his 'call' by the Muses was not meant to be taken seriously; it is a mocking reminder of Hesiod's serious claim. This mockery of convention and frank insistence on reality is one of the clearest traits in Archilochos. To a highly respectable Athenian like Plato's uncle, the odious Kritias [20], it was extremely shocking: 'If he had not published such accounts about himself, we should not have known either that his mother was the slave Enipo, or that poverty and want made him leave Paros for Thasos, or that he then got himself hated by the Thasians, or that he abused his friends and foes equally. In addition, if he had not told us, we should not have known that he was an adulterer or that he was lustful and violent, nor what is the most disgraceful of all, that he threw away his shield.' To throw away one's shield and save one's life was incorrect conduct for a hoplite, and Archilochos makes it worse by giving his shield the Homeric epithet 'blameless' and saying that he can get another equally good [21], and in another poem he expresses an idea which may also have formed the conclusion of the shield poem (64): 'no man has much reverence or fame from his fellows when he is dead. We living seek the favour of the living. The dead always come off worst.' Again the heroic ideal of immortality by fame is shown to be nonsense. It is part of his realistic philosophy that some disasters cannot be avoided. This recognition of the ebb and flow of human fortunes has various consequences. A disgrace may be frankly stated but must not be concealed [22]. Excessive joy or pride in good fortune or wealth is as unsuitable as excessive sorrow in disaster, for which the gods have provided an antidote in Endurance [23]. This is not resignation but strength. The lesson to be drawn from the mutability of human fortunes is that the bad is as impermanent as the good, and therefore one can live positively to the height of one's power: 'one big thing I know, how to return evil for evil [24].'

The other powers that he claims (and it is remarkable how often he uses the phrase 'I know how to') are first the ability to write poetry [25]; 'Under arms my bread is baked, under arms my Ismaric wine, under arms I lie and drink; I am the servant of Lord Enyalios *and* I know the lovely gift of the Muses.' The

gift of the Muses was quite literally, as his hearers would know,
the lyre which they had given him. In another poem he claims:
'I know how to lead the lovely song of Lord Dionysos, the
dithyramb, when my wits are fused by the thunderbolts of
wine.' The last phrase should not be used as evidence either for
Archilochos' state of mind when composing the dithyramb or
for the kind of dithyramb which he wrote; it is a piece of mock-
heroic swagger like his 'call' by the Muses. An inscription tells
us that he introduced against opposition a new cult of Dionysos,
which will concern us in the next chapter, and his claim to sing
the dithyramb may be connected with this [26]. He claims also to
interpret social behaviour and with his typical swagger gives
Zeus as his authority [27]. Above all he claims to give political
advice: 'My forlorn fellow-countrymen, listen to my words,'
'Let not the stone of Tantalos hang over this island . . . You are
all mad,' 'Erxies, why is the luckless army mustered again? . . .
These things my soul in anger (draws up) from the bottom of
my heart . . . realize now, if (you can understand my) words [28].'

Archilochos had no doubt of the importance of what he had
to say, but he had to ensure that it was remembered. This is
partly achieved by his swagger; in other terms, he reminded his
audience of Homeric poetry and heroic convention and contrasted himself with it, so that if they remembered the epic or
their traditional standards they would also remember him. By
this technique of epic reminiscence he made his own youthful
love memorable [29]: 'Such a passion of love wound itself beneath my heart, poured thick mist over my eyes, and stole the
tender wits from my breast.' His love wound itself beneath his
heart with the relentless intensity of Odysseus winding himself
beneath the shaggy belly of the ram to escape from the Cyclops'
cave; it caused a mist as thick as the mist poured over Achilles'
eyes by Poseidon when he rescued Aeneas from destruction; it
stole his youthful wits as a lion eats the tender heart of a deer.
Small is compared to big and becomes memorable because the
big is so well known.

Archilochos also found in the epic another method of making
his poetry memorable. Homeric animal similes are short
stories about animals introduced as working models of the
situations which they illustrate. Animals have a fixed value—
lions are strong and kingly, deer are swift and cowardly, foxes

are clever—and stories are easily remembered³⁰. The Parians
liked animals; witness the long-legged deer on the Parian vase
in Stockholm. Archilochos identified himself with the cunning
fox who always wins the last round, and the long-haired, long-
legged, but, as he thought, gutless Glaukos with the deer³¹.

One of these poems can be reconstructed in its main out-
lines³². Archilochos was engaged to Neoboule the daughter of
Lykambes, to whom he had presumably done some service.
Lykambes at a late stage refused to allow the marriage, and
then evidently performed some action which gave Archilochos a
chance of attacking him and his children. I give the fragments
in the order which seems to me most likely with the minimum
of connecting links: 88 'Father Lykambes, what is this you have
planned? Who twisted your wits which were so firm before?
Now you are the mockery of the town.' 88A 'You have caught
a cricket by the wing' (the cricket is the poet and sings even
more loudly when caught). 89 'There is a well-known story
that a fox and an eagle made a compact.' They decided to live
near each other, but the eagle carried off the foxcubs 'and set
them before his children, a baneful feast' (90). The fox com-
plained, but the eagle answered, 'You see where that high crag
stands rugged and malignant. There I sit, making light of your
warfare (92a) . . . I will not cease to remember my lonely
children as I carve my path swiftly through the air and whirl my
light wings. But your soul hopes . . . ' (*Ox. Pap. 2316*). The fox
hopes to find some way to damage the eagle (91), but has no
'light wings to whirl' (92b); she prays to Zeus: 'Zeus, father
Zeus, thine is the power in heaven, thou overseest the works of
men, their violence and their lawfulness. The just and unjust
dealings of men are thy care' (94). Zeus heard the prayer as the
sequel shows. The eagle seized a piece of meat from the altar
of Zeus, and carried it up to its nest: 'for two fledglings and
itself lived on a crag high above the earth in a nest of straw. To
them the eagle gave the evil gift that they might have food'
(*Ox. Pap. 2315*), but the meat had still a spark of fire in it (94a)
which set fire to the nest; the fledglings dropped into the jaws
of the fox. The poem probably ended with a return to Lykambes: 'You cared nothing for the great oath you swore, the salt
and the board you shared' (95).

Disregard of the conventions of aristocratic society, ruthless

exposure of his enemies and of himself, combined with a belief
that man can endure his misfortunes, a certainty in his own right-
ness and a remarkable power of blistering, economical verse
makes Archilochos the first of the Angry Young Men. He himself sang for a comparatively small circle in Paros and Thasos,
but his violence and vigour ensured that he would be sung even
where the objects of his scorn meant nothing. Before his force
his contemporaries and successors appear pale; but it must be
remembered that much seventh-century elegiac poetry was not
meant to be individual in the sense that Archilochos is nearly
always individual. Some of it is poetry to be sung by hoplites
on the march, some of it is poetry sung at drinking parties:
pretty, pensive, sometimes hortatory, and sometimes despond-
ent [33]. In Solon again we find a great individual, nearer to
Hesiod than Archilochos because he is not inspired by personal
hatred of individuals, nearer to Archilochos than Hesiod because he had an established position in a community which
could act on his advice. Whether he was poet first and therefore
statesman or whether he was statesman first and found his
poetry a convenient means of making his political views accept-
able, we perhaps cannot say. His political place as the founder of
Athenian democracy needs no elaboration here. Plutarch [34]
tells the story that when the Athenians had failed in a long war
with Megara for the possession of Salamis and had passed a
law that no one should on pain of death revive the Athenian
claim to the island, Solon put round the rumour that he was
mad, then one day came into the market-place with a herald's
cap on his head, and when a crowd had collected leapt on to the
herald's stone and recited a poem, which began 'I am a herald
come from lovely Salamis with a song in ordered verses instead
of a speech'. Only eight of what the fatuous Plutarch calls the
hundred charming lines survive: 'May I then change my country
and be a Pholegandrian or a Sikinete instead of an Athenian!
For those words will soon be heard in the world: "this man
comes from Attica, one of those who lost Salamis";' and what
is presumably the conclusion: 'Let us go to Salamis to fight for
the lovely island and cast aside our load of shame.' This is a
very special case of the hortatory elegiac poem: encouragement
to fight a particular battle when public mention of it had been
forbidden. It has been suggested that Solon owed his position

as a mediator in the political troubles of Athens to the fact that he was a poet and this was the poet's traditional task, but though we have seen that Hesiod as a poet claimed political wisdom and the right to give political advice, Solon's personal qualities were so outstanding that however much his position as a poet helped him it is hardly necessary to look beyond his personal qualities for the explanation of his eminence.

His political solution was the direct expression of his philosophy, and he was as confident as Archilochos that he was right[35]: 'These things my soul bids me teach the Athenians,' 'I know, and my heart is full of pain.' Solon prays to the Muses for wealth and reputation, but he does not ascribe his wisdom to them; in fact they are only introduced because it was traditional to begin a poem with a prayer to the Muses. The long poem[36] in which he stated his philosophy is individual in thought and striking in expression. Very crudely, his problem was to persuade people not to exploit their weaker neighbours in spite of the obvious fact that the guilty flourish. It was Hesiod's problem which had become particularly urgent in Athens in the late seventh century. His solution is partly emotional and partly intellectual. He starts by frightening his audience with the picture of the spring storm rising suddenly from the sea and ravaging the fields and then sunshine returns: 'such is the vengeance of Zeus.' This is the lesson to be remembered: crime will certainly and suddenly be punished by the gods. The rest of the poem justifies this position: the guilty seem to flourish and the innocent seem to suffer, but this is only because Zeus may punish a descendant of the sinner instead of the sinner himself. It follows that human hopes may be smashed at any time. Solon reviews human hopes of many different kinds, professional and otherwise, showing that the future is unpredictable, and concludes that any gainful pursuit may give rise to an infatuation which will certainly bring divine punishment on the sinner or his descendants. It is therefore man's responsibility to avoid crime in spite of the apparent rewards of crime, and the responsibility is firmly fixed on the individual.

In Solon's political poems no names are mentioned. His contemporary Alkaios[37] of Lesbos takes us back to the practice of Archilochos. In fact the number of people named in the poems of Alkaios is much the same as in the poems of Archilochos: we are back in island politics, in which the poet himself took a considerable and apparently unsuccessful part. The range of subjects is much the same as in Archilochos—the stages in the struggle of his friends to gain or hold power, abuse of the enemy, general encouragement in the struggle, gloom in exile, other political events, abuse of the old prostitute, the drinking party to celebrate the death of an enemy or to cheer his own discomfort [38]. He lacks the fire of Archilochos, and though the political events were perhaps more important and the personalities are better known than those in Paros, they make much less impact on us. Nor do the political allegories of the ship of state or the vine with unripe grapes etch themselves on the memory with the intensity of Archilochos' animal fables [39]. Archilochos recalled Homer only to flout Homeric conventions; but Alkaios retells Homeric stories to please his audience [40]. He lacks the older poet's vigour and economy and power, but he is nevertheless an individual living intensely the life of his island, bitterly resentful when excluded from its political life and aware of its beauties [41]: 'I in my misery live like a rustic, Agesilaidas, though I long to hear the Assembly summoned and the Council. What my father and my grandfather had till their old age in this city of mutual wrongs, from that I am driven out, exiled on the furthest fringes . . . I dwell, keeping my feet clear of troubles, where Lesbian girls trail their skirts in the beauty contest, and around me rings the wondrous sound of the holy cry of women every year.'

Aristotle has a curious reference to Alkaios in the *Rhetoric*, which connects him with Sappho [42]. He is explaining that people are ashamed if they speak or do or propose shameful things, and he continues 'as Sappho wrote, when Alkaios said "I want to say something but shame prevents me", "But if you had any desire for the noble and the good and your tongue were not confounded with speaking evil, shame would not have bound your eyes but you would have said what you claimed".' Aristotle's phrasing seems to mean that Sappho in a poem quoted Alkaios and then answered him, and this is how the ancient commentators on Aristotle understood him: Alkaios was in love with a girl and Sappho introduced the conversation between the two lovers. Alkaios would seem to have sung of his love for a girl who was connected with Sappho, and Sappho answered with a song in which she quoted Alkaios' poem and gave the girl's answer to him. It is simplest to suppose that the girl was a singer trained by Sappho, who was employed to sing at a party attended by Alkaios. We have to suppose that in the ancient world as now parties might be male, female, or mixed, but it is probably justifiable to suppose that the women in mixed parties were professionals, singers or otherwise. Thus not only girls trained by Sappho but Sappho herself could have sung her songs at mixed parties as well as at female parties. There is also one other kind of occasion at which Sappho's songs could have been sung by men; half a century later Anakreon and his companions sometimes wore women's clothes at their drinking parties [43]. This may have already been a custom in Sappho's time, and such a party would provide an occasion for the unique poem by Alkaios in which a woman laments a disastrous love affair [44].

Thus the circles of Sappho and Alkaios overlapped; she seems to have had the same political sympathies and to have paid for them with exile to Sicily. Her brother, for whom she prayed a safe return and final escape from a dangerous woman, probably belonged to Alkaios' circle [45]. But to understand her own circle we must recall the girls for whom Alkman wrote [46]. He was writing for girls who sang in girls' choruses; they had leaders and trainers, and they were bound together by strong ties of affection. The choruses performed in honour of a goddess, and in this sense Alkman's poetry was public poetry. In the same sense the marriage songs composed by Sappho and performed by her girls were public poetry; one other fragment remains of a song about the death of Adonis sung to Aphrodite by a chorus of girls, and in another there is perhaps a hint of a chorus of maidens singing in honour of Hera [47]; yet another chorus of Lesbian women is mentioned by Alkaios in the poem on his exile already quoted. Sappho calls her house a house 'which serves the Muses' [48]; what distinguishes her from Alkman's Hagesichora or Ainesimbrota is that she performed Alkman's function as well as theirs: she not only trained the girls, she also wrote their songs; and she hated her rivals as much as Alkaios hated his enemies, and abused them in far less conventional terms [49].

Alkman described the bonds of affection which united girls and trainer, and these descriptions are found in the public choruses which he wrote for them to sing. Sappho expresses the same emotions in her solo poetry, which we suppose that she sang at their private parties. Alkman [50] speaks of 'a desire which unties the limbs' and 'a glance which is more melting than sleep or death'. The victim is completely overcome by desire. The phenomenon had already been noted by Archilochos [51]; and he, Alkman, and Sappho all quote and elaborate Hesiod's description of love as 'untying the limbs'. Sappho [52] sees a man sitting opposite a girl whom she loves and listening to her sweet voice and lovely laughter; 'It dismays the heart in my breast; for as I look on you a little, no word comes to me but my tongue is held in silence, a fine flame runs under my skin, my eyes have no sight, my ears buzz, cold sweat possesses me, trembling captures me entirely, I am yellower than grass, I seem to be little short of death . . . but all must be endured.' Here the text breaks off and we only know that Sappho gave a reason for her endurance; but whether the girl was to marry the man or not we cannot say.

What makes Sappho so individual is not only the intensity of her emotion but also the art with which she describes it. Here she leads up through the symptoms to the climax 'I seem to be little short of death', which is a direct contrast to the first line 'He seems to me equal to the gods'; mortal pain contrasted with immortal bliss. In another poem [53] she prays to Aphrodite to help her in her love, as she had helped before, when she asked smilingly why Sappho had called her again: this is a delicious perspective of past emotional crises which the goddess has laughingly solved, and the poem is beautifully shaped with the narrative of the past between the opening and the concluding prayer for present help. There is a remote connection with the swagger of Archilochos here; like him Sappho can stand aside and smile at her misfortunes, and like him she can defy convention and prefer Anaktoria's gaiety or her own daughter's flower-like form to all Lydia and its chariots [54].

The story of love poetry (and of abusive poetry) could be continued to include Ibykos, Anakreon, and Hipponax— Ibykos rich and elaborate in style, Anakreon light, witty, and elegant, and Hipponax scurrilous and flat; but all these poets [55] belong as much or more to the succeeding period as to our period, and all in their different ways show much of the sophisticated style of the late sixth century. Nor do they add anything essential to the picture of growing individuality, which is our primary concern. But a quite new expression of individuality begins to appear in the sixth century, which is of great importance for the future. This is the conception of the individual as primarily an individual soul with a possibility of individual immortality and therefore a supreme sense of responsibility for its actions. It is difficult for us both to account for this new development and to phrase it correctly, since all the poets of which we have spoken were highly developed individuals, and Hesiod, Archilochos, and Solon, at least, had a strong sense of moral responsibility. Undoubtedly they were great individuals and they had a strong sense of responsibility; but it is also clear that if a man believes that he is immortal (or even if he only lives among people who believe that they are immortal) he will rate individuality and responsibility highly; that if mental activities come to be rated more highly than bodily activities, mental individuality will be rated more highly than bodily individuality; and that if the control of the universe is vested in a god who is primarily wise instead of in gods who are primarily strong, moral responsibility and mental activity in the individual are again at a premium; lastly that if a single term can be found as a name for the soul in all its aspects which contrasts it with the body, the new conception becomes articulate.

The word which will serve as a guiding thread through this complicated development is *psyche* [56]. This word, which had a greater future than any of the other Homeric words for mind, heart, or spirit, has in Homer the smallest psychological extension. It is the breath blown out in death, which survives in the underworld as a shadowy replica of the man. Because its absence means death, its presence means life, and when Achilles was chasing Hektor round the walls of Troy, the prize for their race was 'not a victim or an ox-skin but the *psyche* of Hektor'. Thus already in Homer *psyche* is a condition of life although it is only mentioned in connection with death; and although its survival after death was unsubstantial and unsatisfactory, it was believed to survive, and its unsubstantiality and isolation

were largely due to the comparatively recent practice of cremation and to the peculiarly unstable conditions which caused the
introduction of this method of burial [57]. It is probable that the
belief in a more satisfactory immortality for those who performed certain ritual acts was very old, and that at Eleusis at
least such a belief was held continuously from Mycenaean
times: this undercurrent of belief came to the surface again
particularly in the sixth century in the various cults which are
conveniently classed together as Orphic [58]. But we have no
evidence from our period that *psyche* was used in religious
contexts of this kind.

The development of the word's meaning can however be
traced in the poets and philosophers. Four passages mention
psyche in connection with seafaring. The first, in Hesiod's
Works and Days (686-7), was probably in the minds of the
other three poets but they made different adaptations of it.
Hesiod writes: 'Money is *psyche* for unhappy mortals, but it is
grim to die in the waves.' *Psyche* here means something like
life-blood, something more positive than the Homeric *psyche*,
but the idea of death comes in the next sentence. Archilochos
(21 D) describes sailors as 'having their *psychai* in the arms of
the waves'; the meaning again is life, and dangerous life if, as I
suspect, we should think of the sea as a step-mother rather than
a mother. Aristeas (1 K) speaks of unhappy men 'with their
eyes in the stars and their *psyche* in the sea'. It is possible that
psyche means not only life but *emotional* life here [59]; certainly
psyche feels emotions in our fourth poem, a sixth-century
Eretrian epitaph [60], which ends 'a sailor, who gave many evils to
his *psyche*'. Thus *psyche* in sixth-century poetry was not only a
living but also a feeling thing. When did it also become a
thinking thing?

The earliest of the philosophers, Thales, seems to have spoken
of a *psyche* in the magnetic stone and in amber, but this does
not mean more than that they exhibit a kind of life, a power of
positive action normally associated with human beings, but
he may also in the same sense have attributed *psyche* to the
whole world, which showed a similar power [61]. More significantly Anaximenes [62], probably about the middle of the sixth
century, spoke of 'breath and air containing the whole universe
just as our *psyche* controls us'. Our text may be paraphrase

rather than quotation, but it is probable that Anaximenes gave *psyche*, which had only been a principle of life in Thales, a new function of controlling both the human being and the world. The next step is taken perhaps rather after the end of our period by Xenophanes [63], whose god is something like pure perception and controls the world by the power of his thought. Xenophanes also proclaims that his wisdom is more valuable to the city than the prowess of the Olympic victor. The old poet had based his authority on the gift of the Muses; Archilochos and Solon had claimed that they themselves had knowledge; Xenophanes was writing in this tradition when he rated his wisdom higher than Olympic victories, which were the supreme prize of Greek athletics and the winners were given fantastic honours by their cities. Here then wisdom is both stated as the highest goal of human endeavour and sanctioned by a new emphasis on divine wisdom.

We do not know whether Xenophanes located such wisdom in the *psyche*, but probably still in the sixth century Herakleitos of Ephesos [64] wrote that 'eyes and ears are bad witnesses to men if they have barbarian *psychai*'; a barbarian *psyche* is a soul which does not understand the language of the senses, and here at last we have quite clearly *psyche* in the meaning of a thinking soul. Xenophanes [65] himself says that when Pythagoras saw a man beating a puppy he told him to stop: 'for it is a friend's *psyche* and I recognized it when I heard its voice'. This is a playful reference to Pythagoras' theory of the transmigration of souls and has from our point of view considerable interest. This *psyche* feels pain and has control over the voice; it is immortal because it passes from life to life, and it is individual because it is recognizable in a new bodily form. It is a thinking, feeling, immortal, individual soul.

Aristeas of Prokonnesos, as we have seen, maintained that he was not bound by the ordinary rules of space and time; he may have used *psyche* to denote the part of him which made these shamanistic journeys, but the only use of the word that survives from him is the feeling *psyche* of the sailors mentioned above. His poem must have been one of the justifications for Pythagoras' theory of the transmigration of souls. The other is the religious belief in the immortality of the soul, and the part of man which survived death was traditionally called *psyche*;

psyche would therefore have been the natural word for Pythagoras to use to describe his immortal, individual, puritan soul, and we can trust the evidence of Xenophanes that *psyche* in fact was the word that he did use.

That rather after the end of our period the ordinary man was aware of this new (or at least newly articulate) conception of an individual soul with a possibility of immortality and therefore a strong sense of responsibility is clear from some late sixth century poetry and the art of the very early fifth century. Take two examples. First, a two line epitaph from Athens: 'Modest, intelligent, hospitable, trustworthy, honourable, in the bloom of youth Xenares died'[66]. All the emphasis is on the moral qualities of the dead man. The second is a poem of Simonides [67] which was written about 514 B.C.; he shows that the normal aristocratic ideals of birth, health, strength, and wealth are dependent on external circumstances; he announces as his own discovery a new ideal, the man pure in motive, who of his own will does nothing dishonourable, a healthy man, who knows the justice which benefits the city. Again the emphasis is on moral qualities and responsibility.

The artist is more modest than the poet. Although artists from the early seventh century sometimes signed their works, they very seldom stated more than their names: very occasionally however they referred to themselves as *sophos* or 'wise', the word applied by Solon to poetry and by Xenophanes to his wisdom, and a vase painter might write 'beautiful' to describe a figure that he had painted or the vase that the potter had made [68]. But in spite of this apparent modesty the achievement of archaic artists in individualization was enormous, since they created not only portrait sculpture of contemporaries but also the normal appearances of gods and heroes, so that they are recognizable even without the inscriptions which archaic painters often supplied to identify them. Figure painting in the eighth century already distinguished between men and women and represented a number of different kinds of action, particularly combat postures, with great skill. Any further individualization was precluded by the style of the geometric silhouette, and although the majority of geometric figure scenes probably represent mythical scenes it is notoriously difficult to say what mythical scenes are in fact represented [69]. In the seventh cen-

tury inscriptions beside the figures were sometimes used to
identify the figures, and they were common in the sixth, but
much more important than the inscriptions was the new swelling
out of the figure to natural proportions with an increasing use
of inner markings within the outline, whether the figure was
drawn in pure outline, as in the early seventh century, or in
outline filled with flesh colour, as on the vases of some fabrics
in the later seventh century, or in silhouette with incised inner
markings, as in the black-figure style of the latest seventh
century and the first three quarters of the sixth.

A few examples (many of which we have looked at already)
will make the development clear. Before the end of the eighth
century the geometric silhouette had filled out considerably, the
head was illuminated by the eye, and women wore elaborate
embroidered skirts [70]. By the middle of the century the full
outline style was used, whether it was filled with flesh colour or
not. Thus in the Argive blinding of Polyphemos the details of
the gruesome act are convincingly shown, and we need not
doubt that Odysseus was distinguished from his companions [71].
The use of outline and inner markings allows so much more
detail to be given that, without any individualization of faces,
clothing and attributes make clear the unique scene which is
presented: in the Cycladic picture [72] of Apollo arriving at
Delos with the Hyperborean maidens, the winged horses show
that he is divine and the lyre that he is Apollo; Artemis is
identified by her bow and arrows. At the very end of the
seventh century and the beginning of the sixth century we can
perhaps speak of individual characterization in the tremendous,
hook-nosed Herakles who slays the Centaur on the Attic
amphora and the grim Achilles ambushing Troilos on a Corinthian bottle painted by Timonidas [73]. Here too the characterization owes more to posture and attributes than to face; much
is added by the enormous Gorgoneion on Achilles' shield and
by the contrast between the waiting warrior and the peaceful
figure of Polyxena drawing her water from the fountain under
the olive tree. It would not be wrong to call this contrast dramatic, and the same adjective might be applied, although we must
remember that the contrast is already portrayed in the sixth
book of the *Iliad*, to the contrast between Hektor, Andromache,
Paris, and Helen on a Chalkidian krater painted late in our

period [74]. Hektor is fully armed in helmet, corselet, shield, and greaves, as he says goodbye to Andromache, who is covered up in veil, himation, and chiton; they are entirely absorbed in each other. Paris makes the most of his fine figure and has his hair done in the latest fashion; Helen has drawn her himation tightly round her to show off her seductive curves, and looks over her shoulder to see the man who is approaching. The whole tragedy of Ajax is expressed in the large eye, the furrow below it, and the two furrows of the forehead, as he fixes the sword in the ground so that he may commit suicide; in this scene perhaps for the first time the Attic black-figure painter Exekias [75] has used the face to express character, not the face alone, of course, for the impression of tragedy owes much to Ajax' posture, to the palm tree, which shows that he is far from home, and to the spears, helmet, and shield, with which he had won his fame. Exekias was a great artist and this picture gives a foretaste of Sophocles.

The vase-painter, of course, also painted his contemporaries [76], and the only reason for concentrating on mythical pictures is that there the story helps us to understand his intention. Much mythological sculpture, as we have seen [77], survives from our period, but for our immediate purpose the large-scale portrait statue or relief is more useful than architectural sculpture. The increased wealth of Greece in the seventh century made stone sculpture possible, and stone men and women were set upon graves or dedicated to the gods, like the long series of marble maidens dedicated to Athena on the Acropolis at Athens or the seated men dedicated to Apollo at Branchidae [78]. The use of grave statues and grave reliefs representing the dead man or woman is itself evidence of the new sense of individualism. In Athens in the eighth century the grave was marked by a small stone slab neither carved nor inscribed and an immense clay vase decorated with heroic scenes. It is something quite new to commemorate the dead with a representation of themselves [79]. These representations are a long way from realistic portraiture, and portraits of individuals cannot really be recognized until the fourth century [80]. But there was a progressive advance towards realism and by the early fifth century the new sense of responsibility was being portrayed. This general advance occurs in all schools irrespective of their local styles, which in the sixth century were strongly marked—emphasis on the architecture of the figure in the Peloponnese, on sharp decorative detail and patterning in Attica, on volume and surface texture in Ionia, and on the quality of the stone itself in the islands. The advance occurs within certain standard schemes which are used irrespectively of the purpose of the statue to serve as a dedication or to adorn a grave: the standing naked male, the standing draped female, and the seated draped male or female are the most important types [81].

Let us look at four examples, all standing males. A small bronze Apollo [82] dedicated by the Boeotian Mantiklos in the late eighth or very early seventh century is not much more advanced than the figures on the Analatos hydria. The geometric figure has filled out a little; eyes are clearly marked; separate locks of hair are indicated; chest line and belt are just shown. In its original state this Apollo wore a helmet and had a bow in his left hand. From the end of the seventh century and contemporary with the Nessos painter we have parts of several Attic male statues; the best preserved is in New York [83]. This is a marble statue six foot high. The Attic decorative sense comes out in the beaded hair, the stylization of the ears, the framing of the wrist bone (and, in another example, of the elbow), of the groin-line, and of the knees. The proportions are much more realistic than those of the Mantiklos Apollo, but within the outline the detail is summarily indicated except where the outlines are doubled as on contemporary vases. From the front the emphasis is on the immense eyes, which were, of course, painted originally, and on the knees: he was 'quick to perceive' and he 'plied light knees' in Homeric terminology. Another very well preserved six-foot boy from the same place [84] was made about 530 B.C. It has been very probably connected with an epigram: 'Stop and pity Kroisos as you pass by the tomb, whom once fierce Ares destroyed in the front line.' It is the tomb statue of a young Athenian, named after the famous king of Lydia [85], and he had fallen in battle. The posture is the same as before, but within the framework flesh and muscles are represented in far more detail and the exaggeration of eyes and knees is greatly reduced. Attic sense for decoration survives in the elaborate treatment of the hair, and the echoing curves of breast muscles, thorax, and groin-line.

The next step forward is to break the posture, and this step was taken before 480 B.C. The very lovely fair-haired head from the Acropolis [86] comes from a statue of which a fragment of the hips has been identified; the muscles of the neck and the fragment show that the archaic scheme has gone: the right shoulder was raised and the body rested unevenly on the legs. The cheerful expression, which I believe to have been court manners in the archaic period, has also gone, and the boy is pensive. For the first time the youth is not shown on parade but relaxed, or in other words he is not a soldier but an individual in control of his destiny. Thus by the early fifth century the sculptors had given visible form to the new ideal of democratic man.

THE INDIVIDUAL AND HIS RESPONSIBILITY

(References to works of art will be found under the appropriate numbers in the List of Monuments at the end.)

1. Cf. *M.H.*, 254 ff.
2. *Il.* 2, 484.
3. *Od.* 3, 267.
4. Cf. above Ch. I, 6.
5. Date, D. L. Page, *Alcman: the Partheneion*, Oxford, 1951, 164. The date in the middle of the seventh century is strengthened by the equation in the ancient commentary, *Ox. Pap.* 2390 fr. 2. with Leotychidas, the Spartan king of the Second Messenian war, and Timesimbrota the granddaughter of Polydoros, the king of the First Messenian war. New poems are added by *Ox. Pap.* 2387, 2388; 2389 fr. 3 links frs. 2 and 89 D. The Partheneion edited by Page is fr. 1 D and is also discussed by Bowra 30 f.; Fränkel, *D.P.*, 223 f.; *W.F.*, 58 f. (*Ox. Pap.* 2389 includes a fragment of an ancient commentary). The passages referred to below are lls. 39 ff., 51 ff., 64 ff.; Hagesichora and Agido are the leaders of Alkman's choir, but I think the bracelets etc., and the other named women belong to the rival choir trained by Ainesimbrota, who holds the same position as Hagesichora in Alkman's choir; he says in effect: 'neither their dresses nor their girls are enough to defend them against us.' Alkman's choir are cousins (52) or at least 'officially' cousins, and are passionately attached to Hagesichora (77, cf. Page, 91). A similar affection for Astumeloisa is described in the new papyrus, *Ox. Pap.* 2387, fr. 3. 102 D 'this gift of the sweet Muses fair-haired Megalostrata showed forth, blessed among maidens' perhaps names another chorus leader like Hagesichora (cf. Bowra, 21; Fränkel, *D.P.*, 221). Yet another may be Timasimbrota in the poem to which *Ox. Pap.* 2390 fr. 2 is a commentary.
6. On Alkman's birthplace, Page, op. cit. 167 f. and more recently Lobel in *Ox. Pap.* 24, 28. Other similar passages: 92-4 D, in the last two the chorus quote Alkman speaking in the first person.
7. *Op.* 646-662. Cf. above Ch. I, 6.
8. *Theogony*, 22 f. Cf. *M.H.*, 272. H. T. Wade-Gery, *Essays in Greek History*, 6 ff., G. Misch, *History of Autobiography in Antiquity*, 73 ff., and K. von Fritz, *Festschrift Bruno Snell*, 32 have no doubt that this is personal experience; F. Dornseiff, *Kl. Schr.* 1, 37 stresses the tradition in which Hesiod is writing, as also F. M. Cornford, *Principium Sapientiae*, 99. On the Oriental sources of the *Theogony* see most recently P. Walcot, *C.Q.* 50 (1956), 198 f. On the Mycenaean dating of such borrowing see *M.H.*, 85.
9. Cf. F. Dornseiff, op. cit., 74 ff. For the text of Ahiquar see *N.E.T.*, 427.

10. On Hesiod's life cf. T. A. Sinclair, *Hesiod Works and Days*, xvi, xxvii f. Hesiod and Perses: *Op.* 34-39; 396-7. Pandora: 42 f. The five ages: 109 ff.

11. Archilochos 94 D is founded on *Op.* 276 ff.; Alkaios 347 L-P, 94 D is very close to *Op.* 582 ff. (Cf. Page, 303).

12. *Theog.* 901-3. Cf. my *Greek Political Interpretations*, 11; V. Ehrenberg, *Aspects of the Ancient World*, 70 f.; and below, Ch IV, n. 21.

13. Arion: Hdt. 1, 24. Other early dolphin rescues: Koiranos (Archilochos 117 D and 51 A 10 D), Phalanthos (Alkaios 7 L-P, 121 D).

14. Aristeas, fragments in G. Kinkel, *Epicorum Graecorum Fragmenta*. C. M. Bowra, *C.Q.* 50 (1956), 1 interprets the fragments and gives the ancient references. I have confined myself to what is found in Herodotos 4, 13-16. Herodotos dates him in the early seventh century (cf. Wade-Gery, *Poet of the Iliad*, 75). Fränkel, *D.P.*, 319 f. emphasizes the connection with later geographers. Dodds, *Greeks and the Irrational*, 141 discusses Shamans. For a photograph of a modern Siberian Shaman compared to a winged Kalchas in an Etruscan mirror, see J. D. Beazley, *J.H.S.* 69 (1949), 5, fig. 3.

15. The chronology of Archilochos is established by F. Jacoby, *C.Q.* 35 (1941), 97 f. My references are to E. Diehl and R. Beutler, *Anthologia Lyrica Graeca* 3, fasc. 3, Leipzig, 1952 (=D), to which must be added *Oxyrrhynchus Papyri* (=*Ox. Pap.*), 2 (1954), 2310-2319 (comments by W. Peek, *Philologus* 100 (1956), 1 f. and *Wiss. Zeitschr. Halle* 5 (1956), 189 f.; F. Lasserre, *M.H.* 13 (1956), 226; F. R. Adrados, *P.P.* 46 (1956), 38); and the new Parian inscription edited by N. M. Kondoleon, *A.E.* 1952, 58 f. (comments by W. Peek, *Philologus* 99 (1955), 4 f., G. Tarditi, *P.P.*, 47 (1956), 122, and further notes by N. M. Kondoleon, *Philologus* 100 (1956), 36; H. W. Parke, *C.Q.*, 8 (1958), 90). For these new texts I have added a reference to the new Budé text by F. Lasserre (=L), which includes them. Much help is to be found in H. Fränkel, *D.P.*, 182 ff., *W.F.* 55 ff.; B. Snell, *Entdeckung des Geistes* 3, 1955, 87 ff.; F. Lasserre, *Epodes d'Archiloque*, 1950 (quoted below as Lasserre).

16. The story is in the new Parian inscription (cf. n. 15), A II, 22 f. (L, *Testimonia*, 11a). A III, 9-15 (L, *Testimonia*, 12) gives remains of iambic lines and 'lyre' in 1. 14 ensures that the poem recounted this story; fr. 48 may come from an earlier part of the same poem—Archilochos is told by his father to fetch the cow.

17. Herakleitos of Ephesos, writing in the late sixth century, says that Archilochos should, like Homer, be expelled from the contests (*VS* B 42). Kratinos' *Archilochoi* was a comedy quoting and parodying Archilochos. Archilochos' call to poetry was represented on an Athenian vase of about 460 (Beazley, *A.R.V.*, 458 interpreted by Kondoleon, loc. cit). Kritias evidently had read much of him, *VS*, B 44; Plato's Ion could recite Archilochos (*Ion* 531a).

18. Naxos poems: 51, I A, 55 with *Ox. Pap.* 2313, fr. 2 (L 101); 62 with new inscription, B I, 14 ff. (L 80-81).

Thasos poems: 18; 19; 51, I A, 45; 51, IV A, 46 with *Ox. Pap.* 2313, fr. 3a (L 106-10); 62 with new inscription, B I, 14 ff. (L 80-81).
Shipwreck: 7; 10; 11; 12 (with Fränkel, *D.P.*, 196).
Elections: 9; 85 (with Lasserre, 122).
Prostitutes: 15; 25-28; perhaps *Ox. Pap.* 2314, Col. I (on the text cf. A.M. Dale *Lustrum* 2 (1957), 8). On 25-28 cf. Lasserre, 140 f. but note that, whatever the reading at the end, 27 can only be scanned as an iambic trimeter. I doubt Marzullo's ingenious interpretation of 25 (*Rh. Mus.* 100 (1957), 68). 26 may now be identified with *Ox. Pap.* 2311 fr. 1a 5-6 (L 38) and fr. 1 b 7 may fix 36 in the same poem, cf. Adrados for reading, and Lasserre on L39 and 20.
Profligates: 78 (Perikles cf. fr. 7), 102; 107.
Scandalous marriage: 74 is now increased by *Ox. Pap.* 2313, fr. 1 a (L82), which shows that a father, who after an eclipse is surprised at nothing, is faced with the marriage of his daughter. It is probable but not absolutely certain that his name was Archenaktidas and presumably the son-in-law is called *-etos*. These new names seem to exclude the identification of the father with Lykambes (Diehl etc.) or Telesikles (Lasserre).
Love: 71, 72 with 24; 104; 112-117 (see below); 118 with 20 (Lasserre, 165 f.); *Ox. Pap.* 2310, fr. 1 (L 35), Peek takes 1-39 as two poems and at first sight 1. 22-39 on the return of a friend from Crete seem to have nothing to do with 1. 1-21, in which Archilochos answers a woman who has accused him of cowardice. But there is no mark in the papyrus to separate them, although the following poem is clearly marked off from 1. 39. Lasserre, Adrados, and Latte (*Gnomon* 27 (1955), 493) therefore interpret the whole sequence as a single poem, but their interpretations are widely different.

19. General encouragement: 3, 4, 56, 56A, 57.
20. Kritias cf. above n. 17. Tarditi, *op. cit.* n. 15, doubts that Enipo was a slave, perhaps rightly.
21. 6, with Snell 90; Fränkel, *D.P.*, 188; Gigante, *P.P.*, 48 (1956), 196. Cf. 5 for drinking when on guard; 13, 39, 40 (Lasserre 105) Archilochos as a mercenary; 61, seven killed and a thousand claim to have killed them.
22. 58 (Snell, 98; Fränkel, *D.P.*, 186); 67 (Snell, 102); 68 (Snell, 87); 73; *Ox. Pap.* 2317.
23. 67 (cf. Snell, *Gymnasium*, 65 (1958), 48); *Ox. Pap.* 2314, Col. II, 7; 22-3, (Snell, 89; Fränkel, *D.P.*, 190; *W.F.*, 57), the Thasian carpenter's scorn of the wealth and power of Gyges must have been followed by an attack on some local rich and powerful man, whom Archilochos hated. Lasserre (218 ff.) suggests that 18 belongs to the same poem.
24. 66. The sentiment is repeated (with the addition 'and to requite friendship with friendship') in *Ox. Pap.* 2310 fr. 1, 1. 14 f., which confirms Lobel's interpretation of *myrmex* as the worm that turns (cf. above n. 18).
25. The construction of 1 becomes clear if it follows immediately on 2, as I have translated it. Fränkel (*W.F.*, 56) shows that the poet in 1

is more important than the warrior; Bowra (*A.F.C.*, 1953, 27) explains the structure of 2.

26. Dithyramb, 77, for the terminology cf. 76. See Pickard-Cambridge, *Dithyramb etc.*, 5, 18. The inscription, Kondoleon, loc. cit., A III, 1. 16 f. (L, *Testimonia*, 12). The story includes a brief quotation from a poem (32 f.) apparently in hexameters; fr. 34 could come from an iambic poem in which Archilochos told the story. Cf. below n. 27. Tarditi (op. cit. n. 15) argues for a fourth century Delphic life of Archilochos, but the fragments seem to show that the story originated from Archilochos' poems.

27. 41, now extended by *Ox. Pap.* 2310, 41 f. (L 36) which shows that the examples of different pleasures are all regarded as disgusting (84 may belong to a similar claim to be the mouthpiece of Zeus). If Col. II, 37-9 (L37) is rightly identified with 30 D, the prayer to Apollo may conclude the poem. Adrados completes col. II, 43 with fr. 128 Bergk but this is metrically impossible. A poem satirizing sexual pleasures and concluding with a prayer to Apollo to 'harm and destroy them in thy wonted way' may have some relation to the opposition to the new Dionysos cult, particularly as Macrobius shows that Apollo was invoked here to cause disease.

28. 52; 55, now combined with P. London 487 (D, p. 71, 2) and *Ox. Pap.* 2313 fr. 8b and 10 (L 126); 62 suggested by Peek as the first line of the poem in the new inscription, B I, 14 ff. (L 80-81).

29. 112, the Homeric parallels are quoted in Diehl's apparatus, cf. Harvey, *C.Q.* 7 (1957), 214. Snell (93) adds *Il.* 14, 217, where persuasion (one of the charms in Aphrodite's girdle) 'steals the mind even of the wise'. 112-16 come from a single poem contrasting an old woman in the present with the past when the young Archilochos loved her; Lasserre (139 ff.) adds 117 (which may be merely an indication of date) and 27, 34, 106 (but these are metrically discordant).

30. On Homeric similes see *M.H.*, 222 ff. On fixed characteristics in animals see Fränkel, *D.P.*, 200. Archilochos' animals are identified with particular men; rather later Semonides (at great length and much less interestingly) classifies types of women by their likeness to animals (Semonides, 7 D, Snell 278; Fränkel, *D.P.* 269 f.).

31. Parian vase: no. 88, fig. 2. On the fox cf. Bowra, *C.Q.*, 34 (1940), 26 on fr. 103. Lasserre shows great ingenuity in reconstructing Archilochos' animal poems from the fragments and the later echoes of them. His equation (78 f., 104 f.) of Glaukos with the deer is probable. In the story of the fox, lion, and deer the deer is unworthy to succeed the lion because he has no courage (96 D). In another poem Archilochos dislikes a tall, striding, long-haired general and demands a small man with crooked shins but firm on his feet and full of heart (60 D) —the opposite of the deer. The equation with Glaukos is given by another half-line: 'Sing of the well-coiffed Glaukos' (59 D). Glaukos seems to need encouragement in other fragments (56, 68, cf. also 13). His memorial has been discovered in Thasos (J. Pouilloux,

B.C.H., 79 (1955), 75; W. Peek, *Griechische Versinschriften*, no. 51a, but it can only be made into verse by wanton emendation).

32. I have in the main followed Lasserre, 32 f., but I have added the two new papyrus fragments (L 170, 173) and omitted frs. 29, 45, 87, 101 about which I feel no certainty.

33. On the functions of the early elegiac see C. M. Bowra, *Early Greek Elegists*, 1 ff.; H. Fränkel, *D.P.* 208, 209 f., 276 f. Military elegies: Kallinos, 1 D; Tyrtaios, *passim*; Mimnermos, 13 D as interpreted by Fränkel; 12, 12A, 14 may also be historical references from hortations. Sympotic elegy; the rest of Mimnermos.

34. Plutarch, *Solon* 8: the fragments of the poem 2 D, cf. Fränkel, *D.P.*, 290. On the relation between the poet and the statesman cf. J. S. Morrison, *Durham University Journal*, 1949, 59. On the immediate situation cf. A. French, *J.H.S.*, 77 (1957), 238 f.

35. 3, 30; 4 D.

36. 1 D; cf. C. M. Bowra, *Early Greek Elegists*, 90 f.; Fränkel, *D.P.*, 307; Webster, *Greek Interpretations*, 15 f.; the spring storm, above Ch. I, 14. The same philosophy applied to the political situation, 3 D, with similar memorable imagery 11, 14, 19, 28, 32 f.

37. Alkaios cf. Bowra, 145 ff.; Page, 149 f.; Fränkel, *D.P.*, 253; *W.F.* 52 ff. Texts are quoted by the running numbers of E. Lobel and D. L. Page (=L-P), *Poetarum Lesbiorum fragmenta*, Oxford, 1955, and of Diehl (=D).

38. The struggle: cf. Page, 149 f., 161 f. (with reservations by A. W. Gomme, *J.H.S.*, 77 (1957), 255); Snell, *Gymnasium*, 65 (1958), 48 ff. Note particularly 70 L-P (=43 D), 75 L-P (=48 D); 112 L-P (=35 D); 129 L-P; 130 L-P; 296 L-P (cf. P. Maas, *C.R.*, 70 (1956), 200); 348 L-P (=87 D); 357 (=54 D), the armoury of Alkaios and his friends; I see no reason to follow Page (209) in thinking that the armour is old-fashioned: for the plumed helmet cf. the Fikellura Ares, no. 95 and other examples quoted *Manchester Memoirs* 82 (1937), 12. Other events: 45, 48, 69, 350 L-P (=77, 82, 42, 50 D); on 77 D, cf. Fränkel, *W.F.*, 97. Old prostitute: 73 L-P (=46 D), cf. Page, 189, who is over subtle on the imagery. Drinking songs: 332 (death of Myrsilos), 38, 50, 335, 338, 346, 347, 362, 368 L-P (=39, 73, 86, 91, 90, 96, 94, 92, 99 D).

39. The ship: 6 L-P (=119, 120, 122 D); 326 and 208 L-P (=46a D); Page, 182, 186. The vine: 119 (=117 D), cf. Bowra, 182, Page, 242.

40. 42, 44, 283 L-P (=72, 74 D).

41. 130 L-P, Page, 198 f.

42. Ar. *Rhet.* 1367 a 7. Text and commentary are quoted on 137 L-P (=149 D) by Page, 104. It is presumably this poem that was in the mind of the Attic vase painter when he drew (about 470) Alkaios standing before Sappho with lowered head while she moves away from him (Munich 2416, Beazley, *A.R.V.* 260/27, Pfuhl, fig. 772; Schefold, *Bildnisse*, 54). The anonymous line 'violet-wreathed, holy, sweet-smiling Sappho' (Alkaios 384 L-P; 63 D; Page, 108 n. 1; G. Zuntz,

Mus. Helv. 8 (1951), 15) is sometimes said to be Alkaios' address to Sappho; but, 1) it is not quoted from Alkaios, 2) it will not scan even in its present emended form because the name of Sappho begins with a double consonant, as is shown by her use of it in her own poems and by an Attic vase of 510/500 (Goluchow, 32; Beazley, *Vases in Poland,* 9; Schefold, *Bildnisse,* 14): although the spelling with *S* instead of *Ps* was known in Athens by 470 (the Munich vase) the co-incidence of the sixth century vase with the texts of Sappho must be respected. I suspect that the last word of the line was originally *Aphrodite* and not Sappho, and that in its present form it may be a parody by an Attic comic poet. On Sappho in general see Bowra, 186 f.; Page, 3 f.; Fränkel, *D.P.* 230 f.; *W.F.* 40 f., 90 f.

43. Vases and texts are discussed by A. Rumpf, *Studies presented to D. M. Robinson,* II, 84 f.; J. D. Beazley, *Attic Vase paintings in the Museum of Fine Arts, Boston,* II, 55f., two further examples, Riccioni, *R.I.A.,* 5-6 (1956-7), 34, fig. 7, 39-40. The earliest vase is earlier than the pictures of Anakreon and dates from about the middle of the sixth century (C.V., Rhodes, pl. 19, 1-2).

44. Alkaios, 10 and 380 L-P (=123 and 68 D), Page, 291.

45. Political sympathies and exile, cf. Page, 224 f. Relevant fragments are 71, 98 L-P (=70 D). Her brother: 5, 15 L-P (=25-6 D); Page, 45 f.; Gomme, *J.H.S.,* 77 (1957), 258. The ancients (after Herodotos) confused Rhodopis the courtesan of Naukratis with Doricha. The poem, particularly 1. 3 and the final stanza, suggests that Doricha is in Lesbos and that Sappho says 'may he come back and find happiness and may Doricha find that he does not seek her out again'.

46. Cf. above n. 5. Egyptian parallels, F. Dornseiff, *Kl. Schr.* i. 189. On Sappho, Page, 140 f. I agree with the reservations expressed by Gomme, *J.H.S.,* 77 (1957), 259 n. 13 and 260. A. J. Beattie (*Mnem.* 9 (1956), 109 f., *C.Q.,* 7 (1957), 180) seems to me unsuccessful in his attempt to make the emotions expressed in Sappho 1 and 31 L-P (=1 and 2 D) heterosexual.

47. Cf. above Ch. I, n. 37. The maidens who worshipped Hera: 17 L-P (=28 D), Page, 58.

48. 150 L-P (=109 D). The word implies, I think, worship, but the primary service was composing poetry and training singers. I agree with Page that we have no reason to suppose that the instruction embraced anything beyond poetry and music.

49. e.g. 57, 55, 133 L-P (=61, 58, 144 D), Page, 133 f.

50. Alkman, *Ox. Pap.* 2387 fr. 3, ll. 7-8. The glance melts its recipient and captures him as completely as sleep and death: the point of comparison is the complete submission of human beings to sleep and death, and death (bringing with him his brother sleep) is introduced because the lover feels himself near to death.

51. Archilochos fr. 104, 112, 118 D (cf. above n. 29 on 112 D).

52. 'Untying the limbs,' Hesiod, *Theog.* 120 ff.; Sappho, 130 L-P (=137 D), Page, 136; Snell, *Entdeckung,* 95. The lover near death or desiring death; Sappho 31 L-P (=2 D) cf. Page, 19 f.; Fränkel, *D.P.,* 238;

Snell, *Entdeckung*, 94; R. Merkelbach, *Philologus*, 101 (1957), 1 f. Cf. also 94 L-P (=96 D); 95 L-P (=97 D). The poem quoted is, of course, not a wedding song, but the occasion may be the departure of one of Sappho's girls to get married. Fränkel, *W.F.*, 40 f. notes very well how characteristic of Sappho the atomizing style of short sentences is; cf. the marriage of Hektor and Andromache, 44 L-P (=55 D).

53. 1 L-P (=1 D); Page, 2 f.; Fränkel, *D.P.*, 241., *W.F.* 48 ff. I believe Sappho thinks of a particular seated statue of Aphrodite in 1. 1, just as she thinks of a particular temple in 2 L-P. The other interpretation 'with coloured flowers (on thy robe)' (cf. G. H. Bolling, *A.J.P.*, 79 (1958), 275 f.) seems to me less good but possible, cf. the slightly earlier Aphrodite statue, no. 9, fig. 5.

54. Anaktoria: 16 L-P (=27 D); Page, 52; Fränkel, *D.P.*, 250; *W.F.*, 90 ff.; Snell, *Entdeckung*, 88. Beautifully constructed with the return in 1. 19-20 to the cavalry and infantry of 1. 1. The thread is: 'some find cavalry, some infantry, some ships the fairest thing on earth, but I say, it is what one *loves*. So Helen abandoned her home for Paris; she *loved* him and Kypris led her; for Kypris can do what she likes with human hearts' (cf. Fränkel) 'and now she has reminded me of Anaktoria whom I would rather see than chariots and infantry.' Sappho's daughter: 132 L-P (=152 D).

55. Cf. *G.A.L.*, Ch. I the Ripe Archaic Period. On Ibykos, cf. above Ch. I, 12. On Anakreon, Bowra, 284 f.; Fränkel, *D.P.*, 378; *W.F.* 59 ff. Add now *Ox. Pap.* 2321, 2323, with Peek, *Wiss. Zeitschr. Halle*, 5 (1956), 196 ff. On Hipponax, Fränkel, *D.P.*, 284 ff.

56. Cf. D. J. Furley, 'The early history of the concept of soul,' *B.I.C.S.*, 3 (1956), 1 f.

57. *Iliad* 22, 161. On cremation, cf. *M.H.*, 164 ff.

58. On Eleusis and the Orphics, cf. W. K. C. Guthrie, *The Greeks and their Gods*, 281 ff., 314 ff.

59. This is the interpretation of C. M. Bowra, *C.Q.*, 6 (1956), 6, where he also, like Lasserre 237, takes Archilochos (21 D) to speak with the assurance and the affection of a man who knows the sea; I am doubtful of this latter interpretation.

60. W. Peek, *Griechische Versinschriften*, no. 320, cf. (without connection with the sea) the feeling *psyche* in Hipponax 42 D, Anakreon 4 D; probably also Alkaios 117 L-P (=110 D) but the text is too corrupt to be certain.

61. K.R. 91-5 (=*VS.*, A 1, 22, 23). Cf. Guthrie, *In the Beginning*, 47 ff.

62. K.R. 163 (=*VS.*, B 2). Anaximenes' cosmic air seems also to have been divine (K.R., p. 150).

63. Xenophanes' god: K.R. 174-5 (=*VS.*, B 24-6). Wisdom and athletes: *VS.* B 2, cf. *G.A.L.*, 32; Bowra, *Early Greek Elegists*, 127; Fränkel, *D.P.*, 424 f.

64 K.R. 201 (=*VS.*, B 107).

65. K.R. 268 (=*VS.*, B 7). Cf. Fränkel, *D.P.*, 354 ff.

66. Peek, *Versinschriften*, no. 887.

67. Simonides, 4 D; *G.A.L.*, 32; Bowra, 340 f.
68. Wise: Phaidimos, mid-sixth century Attic; Peek, *Versinschriften*, no. 74. Sons of Archermos, mid-sixth century Chiote: no. 24. A vase dedicated on the Athenian Acropolis (Beazley, *A.B.V.*, 351) is inscribed 'men made by their wisdom a beautiful offering'. Solon 1, 53; Xenophanes, 2 D. Beautiful: Attic cups, mid-sixth century, a) Munich. A siren, and beneath it 'most beautiful figure', *A.B.V.* 664 (Beazley however interprets Andrias as a proper name); b) Louvre F 66 'I am beautiful. The cup (or "drink"?) is beautiful.' Beazley, *J.H.S.*, 52 (1932), 178 n. 21.
69. Cf. *M.H.*, 170 ff. mythical scenes in geometric art; 203 ff. geometric figure-painting.
70. e.g. the Attic Analatos hydria, no. 31.
71. Argive Polyphemos, no. 66, fig. 3. Cf. particularly the contemporary Attic Ram jug painter, nos. 35-37.
72. Cycladic Apollo in chariot, no. 89, fig. 4.
73. Herakles and Nettos, no. 40. Timonidas flask, no. 72.
74. Chalkidian Hektor and Paris, no. 87, fig. 9.
75. Ajax by Exekias: no. 59, fig. 10.
76. Miss Lorimer (*B.S.A.*, 42 (1947), 105) speaks of scenes of individual daring and disaster in the hoplite battles on the seventh-century proto-Corinthian vases (e.g. no. 67), and we may add a few striking individuals in archaic painting: Corinthian, the leading dancer Pyrrhias, no. 70; the nameless phallic dancer, no. 76; Timonidas' hunter, no. 71. Laconian, Arkesilas of Cyrene, no. 85. Attic, the fat athlete, no. 58; the victorious lyre-player, no. 61; the rhapsode, no. 63, fig. 14.
77. Cf. above Ch. I, n. 28.
78. For the Acropolis series see H. Payne and G. M. Young, *Archaic Marble Sculpture of the Acropolis* (= *A.M.S.*). For Branchidae etc. cf. above Ch. I, n. 49.
79. On the history of grave-reliefs see K. Friis-Johansen, *The Attic Grave-reliefs*, Copenhagen, 1951, particularly 65 ff.
80. Cf. my *Art and Literature in Fourth-Century Athens*, 16 ff.
81. The series of nude male figures discussed below is Attic except for the Mantiklos Apollo. A similar Attic series of draped females would contain the Berlin standing goddess, no. 5, still showing the tradition of the New York Kouros, and the Peplos Kore, no. 6, foreshadowing the Anavysos kouros, and might close with the Euthydikos kore (Athens, Acropolis Museum 686, Payne and Young, *A.M.S.* 40, pl. 84-8; *G.A.L.* 39, pl. 5), who is the sister of the fair-haired boy and perhaps by the same hand. Contrast with these two series the Island Nikandre, no. 19, and the Cretan-Peloponnesian lady of Auxerre, no. 9, fig. 5, which can be dated respectively just before the beginning and halfway through the second quarter of the seventh century; the Argive-Peloponnesian twins at Delphi, no. 12, which are not very much later than the New York kouros; the Ionian-Samian Cheramyes statue, no. 22, contemporary with the Berlin goddess,

and the head from Ephesos, no. 25, fig. 6, contemporary with the Peplos kore. The Nike of Delos no. 24 probably represents Chiote sculpture about 550.

82. Mantiklos Apollo, no. 1.

83. New York kouros, no. 3. The Sounion kouros (no. 2, fig. 7) and the Dipylon head have long been known.

84. Anavysos kouros, no. 7, fig. 8.

85. For Athenians named after foreigners in the sixth century cf. R. M. Cook, *J.H.S.* 68 (1948), 148.

86. Fair-haired boy, Athens, Acropolis Museum 689, Payne and Young, *A.M.S.* 45, pl. 113-15; *G.A.L.* 39.

III

The Origins of Drama

DRAMA was a new kind of literature invented to meet this new interest in human individuality and responsibility, a new method of presenting the old heroic stories so that in fifth-century tragedy the heroes of the past appeared as men of the present acting and speaking in relation to each other. In Comedy (except for mythological comedy with which we need not concern ourselves) the heroic past was abandoned, and the characters of comedy were either real or imaginary contemporaries. But to say that drama was invented to show the clashes and inter-actions of individuals is to give a final cause, not an origin. The official beginning of drama in Athens took place late in our period. An inscription [1] tells us that in 534 B.C. 'the poet Thespis first acted, who produced a play at the City Dionysia, and the prize was a goat'. This was the official beginning of tragedy; the satyr play was probably introduced into the same festival at the very end of the sixth century, and comedy in 486. Over sixty years of strenuous development separate the official beginning of tragedy from the earliest surviving tragedy, the *Persae* of Aeschylus, and a similar period divides the official beginning of comedy from the earliest surviving comedy, the *Acharnians* of Aristophanes. Much of the early history of drama, as well as the prehistory of drama, is extremely obscure, and all that can be attempted in this chapter is to show what kind of materials, pre-dramatic, religious, or literary, the earliest dramatic poets had to use and what kind of compulsions impelled them towards drama.

If we read, as we now can, a play by the fourth-century comic poet Menander, or if we study his longer papyrus fragments, we find a sort of comedy to which we are well accustomed; and indeed the social comedy of our own day is in a straight line of development from Renaissance adaptations of Plautus and Terence, who themselves adapted the Greek comedies of Menander and his fellows for the Roman stage. The Roman theatre itself was not essentially different from the modern theatre: the stage buildings were connected with the auditorium by side walls and awnings, and the actors were firmly separated from the audience by the considerable wall supporting the stage so that it only needed a darkened auditorium and footlights to produce the picture-frame stage. If however we saw a play by Menander not as it was produced in translation by the Romans nor as it was produced in the Hellenistic theatre with the high stage, but as Menander himself produced it in the theatre of Dionysos, it would look very different.

Most obviously, the relation between audience and actors was quite different when the actors were only separated by a couple of steps from the round dancing floor, which was bounded for half its circumference by the front row of the auditorium. And this round dancing floor, the *orchestra*, was occupied between the acts by the chorus; their songs now were merely interludes; nevertheless some connection with the play was still maintained even by Menander because when the chorus first appear the actors say: 'Let us get out of the way: there are some drunks coming.' Here then Menander was between two kinds of drama: modern drama, where nothing remains of the chorus except the interlude music between the acts, and earlier Greek drama, in which the chorus was present in the orchestra all the time, commenting on or participating in the action, so that it formed both a physical and a spiritual link between the audience and the actors. I should like to say that the link between the audience and chorus goes right back to early, very early times when the village watched the dancers on the circular threshing-floor, praying the god to bless the harvest or thanking him when it was safely stored. Mrs. Ure [2] has recently made this case: the threshing-floor was also the place where the grapes were dried, and Dionysos as the god of wine was naturally connected with the vineyard; there is also a little evidence both in art and literature that Dionysos was sometimes the god of the threshing-floor. It is possible that a circular threshing-floor existed under the Athenian Acropolis in what was later the theatre of Dionysos; or it may merely be that the round *orchestra* was modelled on round threshing-floors elsewhere [3]. In either case the connection between Dionysos, harvest, grape harvest, and dancing place is suggestive and worth remembering, since many elements in Greek drama derive ultimately from agricultural ritual.

The fourth-century poets who reduced the chorus to singing

interludes were using an old element of drama in an entirely
new way. The chorus, which had been the essence of drama,
was turned into a structural device, a means of punctuation.
In the same way masks were a convenient method of showing to
an enormous audience the sex, age, family, social status, and
sometimes the mental characteristics of the characters. By a
further refinement Menander sometimes contrasted the true
characteristics displayed in actions and words with the characteristics assumed from the mask. The state only provided the
poet with three actors so that an actor might have to take
several parts in one play, and the use of masks made this
possible; or a character might be needed in a scene in which all
three actors were already employed, and his mask could then
be worn by a super. In developed drama the mask served the
convenience of the poet; but in origin the mask gave its wearer
the personality of the god or of some being closely connected
with a god, and by wearing the mask and doing what he wished
the god to do, he might persuade the god to act in the same way.
My point here is first to stress that what was invented for one
reason may continue in use because it is convenient for some
quite different purpose (as well as because it is traditional)
and may then be adapted by a genius for an entirely new artistic
purpose; and this, I believe, is a law of very general application.
Secondly, I would note that masks and chorus are elements in
Greek drama whose presence and origin has to be explained.

Let us go back a hundred years before Menander to the time
of early Aristophanes and late Euripides and Sophocles, the
last quarter of the fifth century. What is obvious at once, is that
the plays of Menander are much more like the late plays of
Euripides than they are like the early plays of Aristophanes.
The change from the Old Comedy of Aristophanes to the New
Comedy of Menander took place gradually through the fourth
century; then suddenly someone (the poet Menander or the
politician Demetrios of Phaleron?) realized that the nature of
Comedy had changed, and it was redressed to suit its new
respectability. The Old Comedy of Aristophanes and his
predecessors included various elements which can be traced
back far beyond 486 B.C., when Comedy was officially introduced into the festival of Dionysos—animal choruses, obscene
costume, ugly women's masks, and personal abuse. They have

however all of them something to do with agriculture and the successful bringing to birth of crops, animals, and human beings; for this reason they can all be part of the ritual of Dionysos and we must not forget that the *Birds*, the *Oedipus Tyrannus*, the *Iphigenia in Tauris*, and the *Bacchae* were produced in different years but at the same festival.

At the risk of gross over-simplification we might distinguish five types of play in the late fifth century: heavy tragedy, light tragedy, Dionysiac tragedy, satyr play, and comedy—all produced at the same festival in honour of the same god, Dionysos. Again grossly over-simplifying we might say that a sequence of atmospheres—peace, trouble, rejoicing—underlies them all, but that the emphasis is on different parts of this sequence in the different forms of play. In heavy tragedy (like the *Oedipus Tyrannus*) the emphasis is on the trouble but nevertheless some sort of calm is achieved at the end, and I suppose the same may be said of Dionysiac tragedy, of which the only surviving example is the *Bacchae*; in light tragedy (like the *Ion*), and much more obviously in satyr play and comedy, the emphasis is on the rejoicing at the end; but it is only achieved after a certain amount of trouble, considerable in plays like the *Ion* or the *Iphigenia in Tauris* and recognizable at least in the difficulties which Dikaiopolis has to meet in the *Acharnians* or Strepsiades in the *Clouds*. There is at least a curve, first downward and then upwards, which is common to all Greek plays, however much its steepness and the actual location of its high and low points may vary between them. We have to ask not only whether we can see the germs of these five types of play in our period but whether we can also account for this curve, whether in fact we can see any story or stories of this shape which are likely to have been so important (originally for religious reasons) and so satisfying aesthetically that they established a rhythm or rhythms to which other stories, if they were to be performed dramatically, were made to conform.

Tragedy (as later the satyr play and comedy) was introduced about 534 into an existing festival, the City Dionysia. To this festival also the cities of the Athenian empire sent the grossest kind of fertility emblem, the phallos, as part of their tribute. With other evidence this seems to mean that in origin the festival into which drama was introduced was a festival designed to ensure fertility. This particular cult seems to have been introduced into Athens at a definite moment. The City Dionysia honoured Dionysos Eleuthereus, Dionysos of Eleutherai about 20 miles N.E. of Athens. His image was seated in the front row of the theatre and his temple was just below the theatre. The story was that Pegasos of Eleutherai tried to introduce his cult to Athens. The Athenians would have nothing of it. They then all became impotent and appealed to the Delphic oracle, which commanded them to introduce the cult; the cult included offering phalloi to Dionysos [4]. The temple of Dionysos Eleuthereus at Athens was certainly not built after 500 and probably not much before 600 [5]; at the same time a circular dancing floor was prepared on the site of the later theatre. The introduction of the cult may have been earlier than the temple, but the cult cannot have been old because it was administered by the eponymous archon and not by the King archon, who inherited the religious privileges of the King; this would make a date before the end of the eighth century very unlikely [6].

A very similar story is told in the Parian inscription about Archilochos [7]. He tried to introduce a similar fertility cult in Paros and was opposed. Then the men became impotent, and when they consulted the Delphic oracle they were told to honour Archilochos, which presumably means that he was allowed to introduce the cult. Three of his poems may be connected with this event. The inscription closes the story with a very fragmentary poem in double-short metre which mentions Dionysos, unripe grapes, honey-sweet figs (both perhaps with a transferred sexual meaning rather than in their literal meaning of fruit), and Oipholios, which I take to be the name of a fertility spirit. The second poem, preserved partly on papyrus and partly in quotation, satirizes sexual pleasures and concludes with a prayer to Apollo to afflict Archilochos' enemies with disease; if this combination is right, it sounds very much as if Archilochos' prayer was answered at least to the extent that Delphi threatened them with disease [8]. The third poem survives in the single line: 'I know how to lead the lovely song of the Lord Dionysos, the dithyramb, when my wits are fused with thunderbolts of wine.' As a contest of dithyrambs was later part of the Athenian festival, it seems to me probable that Archilochos' dithyramb was part of this new Parian fertility cult of Dionysos.

Archilochos' working life extended roughly from 680 to 640 B.C. Well before the end of the seventh century the neighbouring island of Chios was making cups in the shape of a phallos and exporting them to Naukratis, Athens, and Aegina [9]; these belong to the same spirit as the new cult. We cannot date the Athenian cult precisely, but it seems likely that it was part of a general movement which swept Greece in the late seventh century.

Eleutherai had curious legends about Dionysos Melanaigis [10], but we do not know that they were imported too. Two Attic vases of the mid-sixth century may well be connected with the phallic cult itself. On a black-figured cup by the Heidelberg painter [11] men dance round a flute-player, wearing long dresses surmounted by an overgarment with a broad central stripe; they have fillets round their heads and beards which look suspiciously false. It is possible that they are the chorus who conducted the phallos pole into the middle of the *orchestra*. The other cup [12] shows the phallos pole itself; it is carried by six men and is surmounted on one side by a giant satyr and on the other side by a giant fat man. These associations are of considerable interest. In the first place the phallos cult is associated with satyrs elsewhere. A late relief in Ephesos [13] shows a large phallos carried by a walking man followed by a man with a tail, who is evidently a man dressed as a satyr. This festival was known as the Katagogia or Return of Dionysos and is evidently the festival to which Herakleitos in the late sixth century B.C. alludes when he says in his dark way: 'they make a procession to Dionysos and they sing a hymn to genitals . . . Hades and Dionysos is the same, in whose honour they rage and celebrate Lenaean rites.' The identification of Dionysos and Hades will concern us later. Here let us note that Herakleitos adds another element to the Return of Dionysos, the wild dances of women known as Maenads; they also will engage us later. They were also associated with the Return at Miletos and at Athens. In Smyrna, Klazomenai, and Athens Dionysos returned on a ship, which was carried or wheeled through the town. In Klazomenai (and therefore probably at Athens) in the sixth century men dressed as satyrs danced round the ship. In Smyrna the festival was called the Anthesteria and was celebrated in the spring. It was in fact a fertility festival: Dionysos as the god of fertility returns to the world in the spring. The

Anthesteria at Athens was much older than the City Dionysia and may go back into the Mycenaean period, since it appears to have spread from Athens to the Ionian cities at the time of the migration. Thus Dionysos already had a spring fertility festival in Athens before the City Dionysia was instituted. He had always returned by sea every year at the Anthesteria. Now, at the City Dionysia, he was brought back by land from Eleutherai to answer some particular need. Formally the festival was new; in essence it was a new form of something very much older, which survived alongside it.

The giant satyr and the giant fat man on the phallos pole at the City Dionysia look forward to classical drama. Satyrs formed the chorus of the satyr play when the satyr play was introduced into the festival at the end of the sixth century, and one common type of chorus in Old Comedy consisted of fat men; the actor of Old Comedy, when he played a male part, was in costume a descendant of the phallic leader of the fat men, whom we know from Corinth (though not from Athens) in the sixth century [14]. The giant satyr and the giant fat man are not simply the creation of pictorial imagination; they are the glorification of actual performers. The fat man is a gigantic version of the padded dancers who appear commonly on Attic vases of the early sixth century, and the satyr is a gigantic version of the men who danced masked and costumed as satyrs [15]. Satyrs and fat men are obviously closely connected, and I think it is probable that the fat men were sometimes referred to as satyrs, but it is better to keep them apart and call them fat men. They are, of course, men dressed up, and where we know their names, as we do from two Corinthian vases, the names suggest that they are men dressed up as fertility spirits [16].

It is well known that the dances of the fat men were very common in Greece in the sixth and late seventh century not only in Athens but also in Sparta and Corinth and Boeotia and indeed all over the Greek world. It is perhaps not quite so well known that, as well as the fat men, men dressed as satyrs appear on Corinthian vases of the late seventh century, that figures like the fat men and the satyrs (but with nothing to show that they are performers) appear on an Attic vase of the early seventh century, that a moulded vase in the shape of a satyr has been found in Samos and dates from the very beginning of the seventh century, that a round dance of ithyphallic goat-men is represented by an Arcadian bronze of the seventh century and a similar single phallic goat-man by a bronze from Samos of much the same date, and that figures extremely like the fat men in posture and shape appear on a relief in Syracuse and on a tomb in Cyprus of the early sixth century [17]. Again these performances were obviously very old and very widespread, and we can now say with some confidence that they went back to the Mycenaean age and were presumably already then connected with Dionysos, since we now know that he was a Mycenaean god [18].

We know one song that the fat men sang, or that was sung by a singer while they danced, because they appear several times in a scene which shows Dionysos bringing back Hephaistos on a mule. Hera threw her lame son Hephaistos out of heaven and he took refuge in the sea. This much Homer gives us, but he leaves out the rest of the story either as being too unseemly or as irrelevant to his immediate purpose. Hephaistos sent Hera a beautiful chair as a present. When she sat on it she found she could not get up again. The war god Ares was sent to bring Hephaistos back but was driven off himself. Finally Dionysos made Hephaistos drunk and brought him back on a mule. On this journey he was accompanied by satyrs and maenads. The reward for Dionysos was admission to heaven and for Hephaistos marriage with Aphrodite. Homer also knows the sequel, the similar story of Aphrodite and Ares, which Demodokos sings in the *Odyssey*: Hephaistos arranges a bed which binds Aphrodite and Ares as unexpectedly and securely as his chair had bound Hera. In one version of the original story Daidalos is substituted for Hephaistos and Enyalios for Ares, and in one version of the sequel also Enyalios is substituted for Ares [19]. Daidalos and Enyalios were the craftsman god and the war god of Mycenaean Crete; it is therefore possible that the story, like the fat men and satyrs who sang it, can be traced back to Mycenaean times.

The story was extremely popular in the late seventh and early sixth century B.C. We know it from vases made in Athens, Corinth, Sparta, Chalkis, Rhodes, and Etruria. In Athens it was sung while men dressed as satyrs danced; in Corinth it was sung by the fat men or sung while they danced [20]. As far as I know, all the groups of vases which have pictures of this story also have pictures of fat men dancing. Later, it was made the subject of a comedy by Epicharmos in Syracuse, which had a chorus of Komasts; they were evidently the Sicilian version of the fat men. Later still, it was the subject of a satyr play by Achaios of Eretria, who wrote in Athens in the fifth century, and the Cretan version was the subject of a fourth-century comedy. Epicharmos in Syracuse probably dramatized a subject which was already sung by the local fat men, and the story may well have been brought there by Arion of Corinth [21] when he made his concert tour of the West. But before he settled in Corinth and wrote songs for the fat men and satyrs Arion came from Lesbos, where his younger contemporary Alkaios composed a hymn in which the story of the Return of Hephaistos was told.

Alkaios' hymn may have been written for the cult of the three gods, Zeus, Hera, and Dionysos, in Lesbos [22]. They are mentioned together by Sappho as well as by Alkaios. Sappho says that the Atreidai did not leave Lesbos after the fall of Troy until they had invoked the help of Hera, Zeus Antiaios, and Thyone's lovely son. Alkaios speaks of a great precinct established by the Lesbians in honour of Zeus Antiaios, the famous Aeolian goddess, mother of all, and Dionysos, devourer of raw flesh. Zeus Antiaios is interpreted as the god of suppliants. The Return of Hephaistos ends with Hera's appeal to Zeus to admit Dionysos to heaven; Zeus Antiaios has therefore a place in the story. In the Return Dionysos is habitually accompanied by his maenads, the wild women who sought communion with the god by tearing to pieces and eating a wild animal; Dionysos is therefore rightly the son of the Rager (Thyone) and the devourer of raw flesh. Most interestingly, Hera is the mother of all, and therefore an earth goddess. This explains the symbolism of the whole story. The binding and release of the earth goddess by the craftsman fire god symbolized originally the binding of the fruitful earth in winter and its release in spring; the craftsman fire god can only be forced to act by the new life of the New Year, Dionysos, who as the result of this act is admitted to the upper world. Thus the story is not only a return of Hephaistos but also a Return of Dionysos like the Returns of the Anthesteria and the City Dionysia.

Both the cult, which we may assume existed in other forms

elsewhere, and the story which explained the cult are surely extremely old, and we need not mistrust the clue which leads back to the Mycenaean age. The story had a great revival, as we have seen, in the seventh and sixth century and may reasonably be regarded with its sequence of trouble, resistance, intrigue, triumph, and marriage as one of the archetypal stories which set the rhythm for satyr play and comedy (and perhaps also for what we have called light tragedy) besides being itself performed in different places and at different times [23].

This long investigation of fat men and satyrs has shown their great age, their renewed vigour in the seventh and sixth century, and their future in classical drama; it has also introduced us to one archetypal story, which influenced the rhythm to which the stories of plays were adapted. But there are other ancient elements particularly in comedy of which nothing has yet been said. What of the animal choruses and the ugly women, who are also a part of Old Comedy, and for that matter the ordinary women like the chorus of the *Lysistrata*, who were not necessarily ugly? The two vases which show choruses of men dressed up as birds are difficult to date and I doubt if we can say for certain that they are earlier than 486, the official introduction of Comedy. The vase with a chorus of Knights, men in armour riding men dressed up as horses, was not painted after 530 and so must be fifty years before the introduction of comedy [24]. Another vase [25], recently bought for Christchurch, shows a chorus of men on stilts wearing a kind of skin breastplate. My colleague, Eric Handley, suggests that they are Giants; but they might also be Titans, and it will be remembered that the chorus of Kratinos' comedy the *Ploutoi* was composed of Titans. So here again we have evidence of a comic chorus fifty years before the official introduction of comedy. There are stories which connect the Titans with Dionysos and these may have provided the subject of their song. But that is guesswork and the important point is that here is yet another early chorus of men in costume. Athenian vases of the first half of the sixth century [26] also show choruses of men dressed up as women dancing by themselves and men dressed up as women dancing with fat men. We can say for certain that all these choruses are part of the background of comedy and satyr play, and that all of them probably performed on an agricultural occasion; but the con-

nection with the festival of Dionysos Eleuthereus itself cannot be
demonstrated, and other older festivals of Dionysos, the Lenaea
certainly and the Anthesteria possibly, included a dramatic
element [27].

The ugly women take us outside Attica because the one clear
case which we know of dances of ugly women is in Sparta, and
these have naturally been connected with the clay masks found
there in the temple of Ortheia. The facts are well known, and I
have suggested [28] that these were dances of ugly women round
an uglier goddess, and that we are justified in seeing parallels
in the big bearded Gorgon masks accompanied by two slightly
smaller beardless Gorgon masks of the eighth century from a
sanctuary of Hera at Tiryns, in the Gorgon-headed goddess on
a Rhodian plate, and in Homer's description of the lame,
squinting, wrinkled Prayers who accompany Infatuation. All
these I take to be dances to promote fertility, but instead of
Dionysos or his representative the centre was a terrifying goddess. At Sparta the goddess was Ortheia, in Elis (the *kordax*)
and in Attica (the bear maidens) she was Artemis, in Arcadia
(Lykosoura) she was the Mistress, at Phigalia she was a horse-
headed Demeter [29]: we do not know who she was in Rhodes or
what Homer would have called her. Homer takes us back to the
eighth century and the Tiryns Gorgons are of the same date.
The fact that variants of this ritual occur on both sides of the
Aegean puts its origin back into the pre-migration period (and
Arcadia was notoriously a backwater where Mycenaean
practices survived) but we have no certain evidence from the
Mycenaean period, as far as I know, for men masquerading as
animals [30] or as ugly women in the service of a fertility goddess.

We can however say that masked dances of this kind were
very old and very widespread. In some of these rites the goddess herself was represented by a mortal wearing her mask—
probably at Sparta, Tiryns, and Rhodes, certainly at Lykosoura
and Pheneos in Arcadia; and at Letrinoi in Elis the goddess
Artemis and her nymphs wore indistinguishable masks. Here
we have the mask used for its original purpose: the human
being becomes the god or rather the god becomes the human
being, and this makes the ritual effective. We know this use of
the mask from Attica itself and, significantly, from the cult of
Dionysos. At a festival, which some regard as the Lenaea and

others with more likelihood, I think, as the Anthesteria, the mask of Dionysos was carefully prepared and was nailed on a tree or pillar with drapery beneath it; under the tree women mixed wine, and I think we may conclude, from the common presence of dancing maenads on the vases which show this rite, that the women sang about the wild dances of the mae-nads [31]. If the festival was the Anthesteria, the mask was presumably worn by the man impersonating Dionysos both when the god arrived in the ship and on the later day when the god was married to the wife of the King Archon. The vases which show the mask and the actual marble masks of Dionysos which survive do not take us back beyond 530 (the frontal Dionysos on the François vase takes us back another forty years and should be derived from a mask); but both festivals were very old, and there are good reasons, as we have seen, for tracing them back before the Ionian migration, i.e. to the eleventh century B.C. The impersonation of Dionysos by a man wearing his mask has therefore a very long history behind it in Attica.

This survey of impersonators who performed during the sixth century and earlier at Athens and elsewhere has revealed much that looks forward to comedy and the satyr play, a little (the Return story) that looks forward to light tragedy and a little (the masked man representing Dionysos and the vase with young men dressed as maenads) that looks forward to Dionysiac tragedy (to this I shall return later), but nothing that looks forward to what we have called heavy tragedy. Few of the Athenian performances which we have considered can be associated for certain with a particular Athenian festival, although they were all there as raw material to be borrowed. We can however, as we have seen, reasonably associate the phallos pole surmounted by the satyr and the fat man with the City Dionysia. It is therefore highly probable that satyrs and fat men danced at the City Dionysia and, as we have seen, one of the songs which they sang, or which was sung while they danced, was the Return of Hephaistos. We may go a step further and suggest that their songs were called dithyrambs, since we know that the dithyramb was later an essential part of the festival, and we have also connected Archilochos' dithyramb with his introduction of the phallic cult. The question then may be phrased thus: by what transmutation could a dithyramb sung by fat men or satyrs develop into an *Agamemnon* or an *Oedipus Tyrannus*?

There is one old suggestion which may now be made more plausible. One of the strange things about classical tragedy is that whereas the dialogue is written in good Attic the choruses are in Doric. It is explained that Doric was the natural language for choral lyric because the great masters of choral lyric in Thespis' time were Peloponnesians [32]. We suppose then that Thespis added an Attic prologue and speeches to choral songs about the heroes of the past written in the Peloponnesian manner. But how could this fit into or grow out of the dances of the fat men and satyrs, which we have come to regard as an essential part of the newish festival of Dionysos Eleuthereus? This would be easier to understand, if in the Peloponnese songs about the heroes of the past were sung by choruses of fat men or satyrs; and this interpretation has been given of the passage in Herodotos in which he describes how the Sikyonians used to honour Adrastos with tragic choruses about his sufferings, until Kleisthenes (in the very early sixth century) handed over the choruses to Dionysos [33]. Tragic choruses have been interpreted as goat choruses, and goats have been equated with fat men or satyrs. Pickard-Cambridge finds 'almost inconceivable' the idea of satyrs and fat men singing of the sufferings of a dead hero. But is it really so impossible? Not if there was any connection between satyrs or fat men and the dead. The new piece of evidence here is the fat man on a tomb in Cyprus, dated in the sixth century. If this is considered with Herakleitos' rather later equation of Dionysos with Hades in the same passage in which he describes the fertility rites paid to Dionysos, with the common appearance of satyrs on tombs from the late fourth century, with the sexual emblems on tombs and in Hellenistic mystery cults, which ensure a successful after-life for their participants, with the fact that a day of the Dionysiac festival of the Anthesteria was connected with the ritual of the dead [34], I think the natural explanation is that Dionysos was always connected with the dead and that the connection is the same as that of Demeter—the corn is buried and rises again and so man is buried and may rise again; then the fertility symbol is no more out of place on the tomb than in the harvest festival, and the

fat men of the fertility cult can sing of the dead without im-
propriety. If this is so, then Kleisthenes was returning (even if
the word should be literally translated 'duly giving') his own
ministers to Dionysos, who had lent them to Adrastos. I use
the word 'lent' on purpose. Our evidence seems to show that
although the great dead of the Mycenaean age were worshipped
in their tombs during the Mycenaean age, the worship ceased
in the dark ages, but was consciously revived in the eighth
century when Greece was becoming sufficiently prosperous
again and sufficiently settled for real (or fictitious) ancestor
cults to have some significance [35]. But there is no reason why the
connection between Dionysos and the dead should ever have
been lost, and so when it became desirable to honour the dead
Adrastos the fat men as ministers of Dionysos were the people
to do it. Then with the new popularity of Dionysiac cults in
the late seventh and early sixth century Dionysos received the
choruses back.

If this is right, sixth-century Peloponnesian choruses of
satyrs or fat men might sing in honour of Dionysos songs
about heroes who had nothing to do with Dionysos. Another
piece of evidence chimes in with this. Arion [36] is said to have
'named' his dithyrambs and was called a 'tragedian' by his contemporary Solon. Named dithyrambs are surely, as later, dithyrambs with titles, and titles probably imply that the range of
subjects included more than the obvious Dionysiac themes like
the Return of Hephaistos. We have seen reason to suppose
that the early dithyramb was danced by fat men and satyrs and
that such dithyrambs were performed at the City Dionysia.
Thus it would not have been very difficult for Thespis to take
over the Peloponnesian dithyramb and its heroic subjects into
the Athenian festival and to convert it into tragedy by the
addition of an Attic prologue and speeches.

It is at least arguable that Arion's dithyramb itself attained
a high seriousness when narrating the stories of heroes. Sometimes, as we have seen, contemporary Corinthian painting
depended on a lyric source, which was almost certainly Arion;
and there is no reason to deny Arion's lyric narrative the power
and dramatic concentration of the best Corinthian vase-
painting, as we see it for instance in the Achilles and Troilos
of the Timonidas bottle [37]. And in Athens itself Exekias' death

of Ajax [38] was painted within five years of Thespis' introduction of tragedy.

G.F. Else [39] has recently reminded us of two important facts which bear on this question. First, the obvious model for the prologues and speeches of the new art form was the iambic poetry of Solon, whose high seriousness and sense of responsibility were discussed in the last chapter. Secondly, the recitation of the *Iliad* and *Odyssey* at the Panathenaea was probably a fairly recent innovation, and these recitations were dramatic in the sense that the rhapsodes delivered the speeches, which occur in large numbers in the epic, with full attention to the age and sex of the epic characters and the position in which at the moment they found themselves. Thus serious dramatic speech was already a known quantity in Athens and had been so since the first recitations of Homer. These various elements of form and content were fused by Thespis into a kind of performance which could in time develop into an *Agamemnon* and an *Oedipus Tyrannus*.

But we have still to speak of another influence which may have been as important for fixing the rhythm and shape of heavy tragedy as the Return story was for satyr play and comedy. This is the Resistance story. By the Resistance story I mean the story, or rather the group of stories, in which Dionysos and his maenads are resisted by a king, on whom Dionysos later takes a tremendous vengeance: the best known instance of the dramatization of this story is the *Bacchae* of Euripides. I believe that Gilbert Murray [40] was essentially right both in finding this kind of story archetypal for heavy tragedy (as well as for Dionysiac tragedy) and in tracing it back to vegetation ritual. The connection between the ecstatic dances of the maenads and the Resistance story is as intimate as the connection between the dances of the satyrs or fat men and the Return story. Dionysos cannot return (whether with Hephaistos or on ship) without his satyrs, and the ecstatic dances of the maenads are the chief cause of the Resistance to his worship. In both cases we have a performance and a story which can be traced back far beyond the official beginnings of drama, and in both cases it is a reasonable guess that the performers often sang (or danced while a leader sang) the local version of the story.

As with the Return story, we can trace both the myth and the

performances backwards. The myth has many different versions
attached to different places and the characters are always
legendary. The Resistance of Lykourgos is well known to
Homer, and there is no reason why these stories should not be
Mycenaean in origin [41]. The performances also were widespread and old [42]. There are many scattered references to
women called maenads or the like honouring Dionysos in
different places during classical and Hellenistic times. In Delphi
they can be traced back to the seventh century. In Ephesos in
the sixth century, as we have seen, they were associated with
the Return of Dionysos, and if this festival was the Anthesteria,
it is likely to have been very old; we have seen also that at the
Athenian Anthesteria the women sang of the wild dances of
the maenads while they prepared the wine at the foot of the
column surmounted by the mask of Dionysos. In Athens they
probably gave their name to the Lenaea, which again was a
very old festival. 'Very old' means before the Ionian migration
and therefore probably Mycenaean. As we now know that
Dionysos was a Mycenaean god, we may see the ancestresses
of the maenads in the women who perform ecstatic dances in
Mycenaean and Minoan art, and these dances have been convincingly interpreted as a vegetation ritual [43].

Thus this strand of Dionysiac legend and ritual leads straight
back to a very early year-god cult of the kind which Gilbert
Murray supposed for the origin of Greek tragedy. In the sixth
century the Resistance story had all the authority of age as well
as the new interest arising from the recent widespread revival of
Dionysos cults. The women who took part in the cults may have
worn fawnskins and carried thyrsoi, but they were contemporary maenads, carrying out contemporary ritual to meet
contemporary needs, even if they sang of the legendary past.
When men dressed up as maenads and represented maenads of
the legendary past taking part in the Resistance story, the trans-
ition was effected from cult to drama or pre-drama. I say drama
or pre-drama because we do not know when this first happened.
Our earliest evidence is an Attic pyxis [44] of the mid-sixth
century, on which a flute-player plays to five youths dressed in
chitons, which come down to their knees, and over the chitons
garments with long tails, which seem to belong to skins. They
formed a chorus of maenads contemporary with Thespis, and

they were either a very early tragic chorus or yet another of the pre-dramatic choruses of which we have spoken. In any case they prove that in Thespis' time on some occasion a chorus of young men did represent maenads, and presumably they sang of tearing to pieces wild animals, if not of Pentheus or Lykourgos. Thus we can make a case for Dionysiac tragedy with its chorus of maenads being a very early form of tragedy [45] which could have influenced the whole development, because the Resistance story (which probably in origin told of the resistance of natural forces to the resurgent life of the new year as a means of compassing their defeat) had become the resistance of man to the power of the gods and his disastrous fall—a story of human pride and disaster to which other heroic stories were readily assimilated, because Thespis and his successors saw their legends in terms of human responsibility.

The early history of tragedy as distinct from the pre-history is still desperately obscure until we can read our first complete play with Aeschylus' *Persae* in 472. What I have attempted to show is that the elements whose development we can trace from Aeschylus to Menander and so to our own day were present in Athens in the sixth century. Thespis drew on Dionysiac cult and legend, Homeric epic, the iambics of Solon, Peloponnesian choral lyric, the dances of the fat men, and the masked impersonators of Dionysos to produce drama, which, however primitive it was in its early stages, showed men acting and speaking in relation to each other. With the opposition of actor and chorus the possibility of development to the agonized decisions, the scenes of persuasion, the extortions of truth, and the character conflicts of Attic drama was given, and the commentary could be put into the mouth of the chorus as one of the participants instead of being given by the poet from his own lips as in epic. In this sense the new art had also a realism unachieved before.

THE ORIGINS OF DRAMA

(References to works of art will be found under the appropriate numbers in the List of Monuments at the end.)

1. See Pickard-Cambridge, *Dithyramb etc.*, 97 (Thespis), 94 (Satyr play); *Festivals*, 83 (Comedy).
2. Ure, *C.Q.* 49 (1955), 225 f. cf. Stricker, *J.E.A.*, 41 (1955), 34. Mrs Ure quotes a fifth-century Corinthian vase on which Dionysos holds a winnowing fan and a winnowing fork. A papyrus of the third century B.C. (*Hibeh* II, no. 177) seems to contain a lament of Semele for Dionysos, and Dionysos is said there to have a golden winnowing fork.
3. The evidence about early performances in the Agora (as distinct from the Theatre) is extremely unclear, and we have no evidence as to the shape of the *orchestra* in the Agora: it may also have been round. The suggestion that the performances at the City Dionysia took place in the Agora before they were transferred to the theatre rests on the assumption that the transference was due to a collapse of the *ikria* (wooden-stands) in the Agora during a performance of Pratinas. The assumption that the *ikria* were in the Agora depends on the connection between the *ikria* and the poplar tree. Pickard-Cambridge is probably right in supposing a) that it was the *ikria* in the theatre which collapsed (since Aeschylus as well as Pratinas was involved) and b) that the early performances in the Agora were connected with the Lenaea rather than with the City Dionysia (*Theatre of Dionysus*, 12 f.). Cf. R. Martin, *R.P.*, 31 (1957), 72 f.
4. The evidence is the Scholiast's note on Aristophanes, *Acharnians*, 243: 'Xanthias, set up the phallos'. Cf. Pickard-Cambridge, *Festivals*, 55 f., 60. The monument set up by the successful choregos (producer) might be phallic in form, cf. Buschor, *A.M.* 52 (1928), 96 f.
5. Nilsson (*Op. Sel.*, i, 128) quotes Wilamowitz for saying that the temple was not earlier than Solonian; Pickard-Cambridge, *Theatre*, 3 says the foundations suggest the epoch of Peisistratos; I. T. Hill, *Ancient City of Athens*, 107, 'before the end of the sixth century'. Stone and technique are identical with the scanty remains of the earliest theatre.
6. Cf. Pickard-Cambridge, *Festivals*, 56.
7. Cf. above Ch. II, n. 26, 27 for references. For Oipholios note that Oiphon is the name of a satyr on a red-figure vase (*A.R.V.*, 25/7).
8. According to Pliny (*N.H.* 36, 4) Sikyon was similarly afflicted in the early sixth century and commanded by Apollo to complete a statuary group by Dipoinos and Skyllis (cf. J. Boardman in *J.H.S.*, 77 (1957), 279).
9. Cf. R. M. Cook, *B.S.A.*, 44 (1949), 158.

10. Reported by the Suda lexicon on Melanaigis, and Scholiast on Aristophanes, *Acharnians*, 146. Nilsson (*Op. Sel.*, i, 113 f.; *Gesch.* 218; cf. Pickard-Cambridge, *Dithyramb etc.*, 160 f.) believes that Dionysos Melanaigis had a chorus of goat-men and finds here the origin of tragedy; but it is not clear that the story or ritual connected with Dionysos Melanaigis was imported with the phallic cult.

11. Black-figure cup, no. 53. The *ithyphalloi* who conducted the phallos pole into the *orchestra* are described by Semos of Delos (Ath. 622) as wearing the masks of drunkards, wreaths, sleeves, chitons with a white stripe, and a Tarantine robe falling to their feet, cf. *G.T.P.*, 36.

12. Black-figure cup, no. 54. Vallois (*B.C.H.*, 46 (1922), 96) compares the elaborate structure of the phallos pole with the terminology of Delian inscriptions which record payments for a similar ceremony.

13. The evidence for most of the statements in this passage will be found in Nilsson, *Gesch.* 543, 550. The Ephesos relief is discussed by J. Keil, *O. Jahr.*, 29 (1934), 91. Sixth-century satyr dances in Samos may be inferred from the large satyr mask with closed lips in the British Museum, no. 28, which is best explained as the mould for a dancer's mask. The Herakleitos text is K.R. 246 (= *VS*. B 15). On the connection between maenads and the Attic Anthesteria see below n. 31. The Athenian ship-car is seen on vases of the early fifth century: Pickard-Cambridge, *Dithyramb etc.*, 114 ff.; *Festivals*, 11 ff.; Haspels, *A.B.L.*, 250, 253. The Klazomenian ship-litter has been identified by John Boardman, no. 94. The essential text for the early origin of the Anthesteria (and the Lenaea) is Thucydides, 2, 15; Cf. Pickard-Cambridge, *Festivals*, 14, 22.

14. The phallic leaders of Corinthian dances are discussed *G.T.P.* 134 and more fully *R.B.* 36 (1954), 582. The Jensen aryballos, no. 76, provides the essential evidence because there is no doubt that the dancer on it wears a large artificial phallos.

15. The evidence for satyr dances in Athens is the not uncommon occurrence of satyrs with frontal faces on black-figure vases (e.g. nos. 48, 52); frontal faces in archaic art can nearly always be derived from masks; this coupled with the occurrence of satyr dances elsewhere makes it probable that Athens also had satyr dances. The evidence for dances of fat men in Athens is discussed *R.B.* 36 (1954), 582: the point which has been questioned is whether Athens itself had such performances or whether the fat men on Attic vases were originally copies of the fat men on Corinthian vases. The strong evidence that the Attic painter was painting a performance that he had seen himself is that one of the earliest Attic vases with fat men, no. 43, shows a padded woman (or rather a man dressed up as a woman) between each pair of fat men; as none of the hundreds of Corinthian vases with padded dancers has a padded woman, the Attic painter must have got his padded women from performances in Athens. Possibly these should be connected with the tradition of Sousarion's comedy, dated between 580 and 560.

16. Add to the names on no. 78, given above Ch. I n. 43, *Eunous* (friendly), *Ophelandros* (helpful), *Omrikos* (rain-bringing?) on no. 77.

17. On dancers from Boeotia, Sparta, Asia Minor, cf. *G.T.P.*, 129, 138, 156. Men dressed as satyrs on Corinthian vases: nos. 65, 77 and 79, fig. 11; cf. also *NC*. no. 1258. Early Attic vase: no. 35. Satyr vase from Samos: no. 20. Arcadian bronze group: no. 10. Samian bronze: no. 21. Relief in Syracuse: *Mon. Ant.* 20, 826, pl. 9 (cf. also pl. 8). Tomb in Cyprus: *S.C.E.*, I, 464, fig. 186; IV, 33 (the likeness was noted by A. Seeberg). Something of the multiplicity of types is inherited by the classical satyr play in Athens. We now have evidence for the following types of 'satyr' in the satyr play: smooth horse-men with smooth drawers, smooth horse-men with shaggy drawers, hairy horse-men (Eucharides ptr., Louvre, below n. 23), old white hairy horse-men (Papposilenos), goat-men (Pandora krater, cf. most recently Beazley, *Hesperia*, 24 (1955), 316).

18. I have given the evidence in *B.I.C.S.*, 5 (1958), 44.

19. Enyalios and Daidalos: British Museum F 269. Apulian kalyx-krater; Bieber, *H.T.* fig. 370; possibly based on Attic comedy, as I suggest in *C.Q.* 42 (1948), 23. Enyalios and Aphrodite: on the chest of Kypselos (Paus. 5, 18, 5). The two stories have been treated recently by M. Delcourt, *Hephaistos*, 78 ff., 85 ff.

20. Cf. *G.T.P.*, 133: the earliest Corinthian vases (e.g. no. 77) are little earlier than the Attic François vase, no. 46, but the Attic picture omits the fat men, while giving a much fuller version of the story. A little later a fullish version on an Attic amphora has a satyr with frontal face (no. 48, cf. 52): the song was then sung while satyrs danced in Athens. The vases are listed by Brommer, *J.d.I.* 52, (1937), 198 and include a Laconian cup no. 86, a Chalcidian amphora (Rumpf, no. 57), two Caeretan hydriae no. 97, and a Campana Dinos, no. 103. The story has also been seen on a Rhodian (Fikellura) vase of the last quarter of the sixth century, no. 95.

21. Cf. above Ch. I, 77.

22. Cf. above Ch. I n. 29, 37. Alkaios' hymn: 349 L-P (=9 D); Page, 258 f.; see also Eisenberger, *der Mythos in der äolischen Lyrik*, Frankfurt, 1956, 27 f. The Triad: Sappho 17 L-P (=28 D), Alkaios 129 L-P; cf. Page, 58, 168. Picard, *B.C.H.*, 70 (1946), 455 f. has an excellent discussion, comparing other places where Hera is an earth goddess and tracing back the triad to a pre-Hellenic origin. Stella in *P.P.* 50 (1956), 321 f. doubts the identification of the two triads. Hera was also an earth-goddess for Empedocles (Snell, *Philologus* 93 (1944), 159).

23. If the essential is the release of the earth goddess in the spring, this is known in other versions, which may also have been reflected in Attic satyr plays: Pandora is released by hammering satyrs (and, strangely transmuted, this story becomes the making of Pandora by the craftsman Hephaistos or of Anesidora by Epimetheus); Persephone rises from the earth and a chorus of goat-men leap round her; Aphrodite rises from the earth and a single Pan looks on astonished. Cf. Buschor,

S.B.A.W., 1937, 1 ff.; later bibliography in *Lustrum* 1 (1956), 104, and J. D. Beazley, *Misc. Libertini*, Florence, 1958, 91, on stamnos by Eucharides painter in the Louvre.

24. Cf. *G.T.P.*, 34 f. The Knights: no. 56.

25. Christchurch Titans: no. 60, fig. 12. None of the Greek words for stilts are relevant except *gypones*, which leads us to Pollux 4, 104 (Cf. Pickard-Cambridge, *Dithyramb*, 258). After describing four Laconian dances, Pollux continues (it is not clear whether he is still speaking of Laconian dances): 'the *hypogypones* represented old men with sticks, and the *gypones* danced mounted on wooden legs'. Wooden legs were certainly stilts; whether the sticks of the *hypogypones* were also stilts is unclear. Before the Christchurch vase was known, I suggested that the man rowing a fish on a late fifth-century Attic oenochoe was a member of the chorus who came in on stilts (the oars) with the fish swinging between them (*G.T.P.* 57; *W.S.* 69 (1956), 112) and compared the *gypones*. It now seems increasingly likely that stilts could be used by the chorus of an Attic comedy.

26. The *ithyphalloi* wore women's clothes but masks of drunkards, cf. above n. 11 and the vase, no. 53, there discussed. The padded women who danced with the fat men I believe to have been young men dressed up, cf. above n. 15 and the vase noted there no. 43. Another Attic black-figure vase of the mid-sixth century has a chorus of youths dressed as maenads, no. 55, fig. 12. Cf. below n. 44.

27. On the date of the Lenaea and Anthesteria see above n. 13.

28. The mid-seventh century Attic amphora in Eleusis, no. 33, has Gorgons who look remarkably like masked figures; if so, an Attic chorus dressed as Gorgons sang of the death of Medusa; but their mask-like faces may be an idosyncrasy of the painter. On the Spartan dances see *G.T.P.* 130. The Ortheia masks, no. 18. The Tiryns masks, no. 8. The Gorgon plate, no. 93. Homer, *Iliad* 9, 502. Cf. also the early Gorgon masks from Gortyn published by D. Levi, *A.S.A.A.*, 33-4 (1955-6), 265.

29. The evidence has been often discussed: cf. Bieber, *R.E.*, s. v. Masken; Nilsson, *Gesch.*[1], 150 f.; *Minoan-Mycenaean Religion*, 503; Wrede, *A.M.*, 53 (1928), 87; Lawler, *Robinson Studies*, I, 23 f.

30. The two likely cases of Mycenaean masks do not belong to this context. One is the possibility that the Minotaur was the King of Knossos impersonating the god in a bull mask; it should be noted that a man wearing a bull mask is known from a sixth century terracotta from Cyprus (*S.C.E.*, II, pl. 233, no. 809), a place where a Mycenaean rite might easily have survived. The other is the mask between two goats on a sealing from Phaistos (*M.H.*, 50; *B.I.C.S.*, 5, (1958), 45), which I take to be the mask of a Mycenaean 'satyr' or of Dionysos himself.

31. Pickard-Cambridge, *Festivals*, 27 f. most recently for the Lenaea; Nilsson, *Dionysiac Mysteries*, 1957, 26 f. most recently for the Anthesteria; he finds a clinching argument in the fact that one of the vases is a *chous*, but it should be noted that *Choes* do not necessarily

carry Anthesteria scenes; his strongest argument seems to me to be the equation (in *Gesch.* 555) of the vases with the text of Phanodemos preserved by Athenaeus 465a, which describes the mixing of the wine and is accepted by Pickard-Cambridge in his Anthesteria texts (no. 20). The vases are discussed with admirable caution by Coche de la Ferté, *R.A.*, 38 (1951), 12. On the masks of Dionysos themselves and on the vases see Wrede, *A.M.*, 53 (1928), 66 f. François vase: no. 46.

32. Cf. e.g. Björck, das *Alpha impurum*, 358: diese konventionell stilisierte panhellenisch verständliche Form lag in der Kantaten und Hymnen der Chorlieder ausgebildet vor. For types of choral lyric cf. Ch. I n. 35-7, 43, 45; Ch. II, n. 42, 44.

33. Hdt. 5, 67. The whole problem is admirably treated by Lesky, *Tragische Dichtung*, 34 f.; cf. also Pickard-Cambridge, *Dithyramb*, 137.

34. Tomb in Cyprus, cf. above n. 17. Herakleitos, fr. 15, cf. above n. 13. Satyrs on tombs: Snijder, *R.A.*, 1924, 1. Phallos on fifth-century Attic white lekythos: Buschor, *A.M.* 53 (1928), 107. Phallos in Hellenistic mystery cults: Nilsson, *Dionysiac mysteries*, 44. Nilsson denies Dionysos any original connection with the All-Souls day on the third day of the Anthesteria, but admits that the festival in its present form may be very old (*Gesch.*[1] 563 f.). I think it is wiser to suppose that Dionysos (like Demeter) had always had this double aspect, but that his connection with the dead was felt much more at some periods and in some places than in others. Cf. Kerenyi, *S.O.*, 33 (1957), 130; Metzger, *B.C.H.*, 68 (1944), 296 f.; K. Friis Johansen, *Attic Grave Reliefs*, 111 f.

35. For the evidence of eighth-century cults at Mycenaean tombs see *M.H.*, 137 ff., 170. For laments sung to heroes see Pickard-Cambridge, *Dithyramb*, 139; Nilsson, *Op. Sel.*, i, 95. Hence the importance of lament forms in tragedy, cf. Peretti, *Epirrema e Tragedia*, 11 f. For laments at ordinary funerals, cf. Ch. I, n. 35.

36. Hdt. 1, 23; Suda lexicon, s. v. Arion; John the Deacon ap. Pickard-Cambridge, *Dithyramb*, 131 f.; cf. also Lesky, *op. cit.*, 29 f. The phrase in the Suda lexicon 'Satyrs speaking verses' has had much interpretation. If Pratinas' later innovation was to make a chorus of satyr dancers into a singing chorus, was Arion's earlier innovation to make a chorus of dancing fat men into a singing chorus?

37. No. 72, cf. above II, n. 73.

38. No. 59, fig. 10, cf. above II, n. 75.

39. *Hermes*, 85 (1957), 34 ff., cf. his *Aristotle's Poetics*, 162 f.

40. *Themis*, 341 ff.; *Euripides and his age*, 64 ff.; *C.Q.* 37 (1943), 46 f. Cf. on the following my article in *B.I.C.S.* 5 (1958), 43, 45 ff.

41. Homer, *Il.* 6, 130 (cf. 22, 460). Cf. Dodds *Bacchae*, xix; Guthrie, *The Greeks and their Gods*, 160, 165, 166 f.

42. Cf. Nilsson, *Gesch.*, 540 ff. On the maenads and the Anthesteria cf. above n. 31.

43. Particularly by A. W. Persson, *Religion of Greece in Prehistoric Times*, 32 f.

44. No. 55, fig. 12, cf. above n. 26.

45. In the early fifth century Aeschylus wrote on the Pentheus story and on the Lykourgos story. Polyphrasmon wrote a *Lykourgeia* in 467 and Sophocles a *Bakchai* in 463 (?). Two vases which can be dated 480/460 show maenads of a tragic chorus: Berlin 3223, *G.T.P.*, 174, no. A 6; Beazley, *Hesperia*, 24 (1955), 312. Ferrara, G. Riccioni, *Arch. Class.* (forthcoming), probably also *G.T.P.* no. A 4, cf. my article in *Hesperia* (forthcoming).

IV

The Beginnings of Philosophy and Science

OUR examination of the history of Greek drama has shown that it was rooted in very ancient religious ceremonies, that within our period a decisive new step was taken, and that drama in the modern sense was achieved with Menander some two centuries after the first official dramatic festival. If we regard Aristotle, as I think we must, as philosopher and scientist in the modern sense, we can draw a similar curve to represent the gradual emancipation of philosophical and scientific thought from religion and magic, and here too the decisive new step was taken in our period, in which fall the lives of Thales, Anaximander, and Anaximenes and the youth of Pythagoras, Xenophanes, and Herakleitos[1]. Of course there was no sudden change, and scholars of the present century[2] have been at pains to emphasize that the achievements of Thales and his successors were much less revolutionary than their Victorian predecessors had supposed; nevertheless a decisive step was taken. The old view that the world had been made and was controlled by gods, who were to some extent influenced by religion and magic and could be expounded by poets and prophets, survived and provided, as we shall see, not only material but also certain tools of thought for the new view; but Thales marks the first step towards the new view that the world is explicable in terms of mechanical models and is therefore more amenable to technology than to magic, and that the scientist's choice of models is based on observations which anyone can check and justified by arguments which anyone can follow and control. It was a momentous change which seems to have begun in Ionia at the beginning of the sixth century: the wealthy individualists of that democratic, pleasure-loving, sensuous, inquisitive civilization chose a craftsman's universe instead of a priest's universe, and Thales, who could foretell an eclipse, measure the height of the pyramids, make a corner in olives, and advise the Ionians to form a federal state, gave it its first tentative expression[3].

We can trace yet a third curve of development which has some connection with the other two: the change in pictorial representation which leads the artist to record and the spectator to accept a three-dimensional view of the world as it appears. The battle of Alexander and Dareios [4], a faithful mosaic copy of an original of the late fourth century B.C., would not look out of place in an exhibition of Renaissance painting; the use of perspective and shading to represent a solid world is convincing, if not final; again the beginning, as we shall see, was made in our period. The realistic artist is like the dramatist in that essentially he reproduces appearances without commenting on them. The dramatist restricts himself to visible actions and audible speeches; the artist restricts himself to visible shapes and forms. He is like the scientist because he distinguishes quite clearly between the world of appearance and the reality behind appearances, but he confines his operations to the world of appearances. The history of art is therefore relevant to our present subject in two ways; it provides evidence both for the abandonment of an earlier magical view and for the increased interest in detailed observation of many kinds.

If we look for a moment at one of the great Attic geometric vases [5] of the mid-eighth century, we are struck not only by the absence of individualization of which I have spoken already but also by the positive conventions which the painter adopts. The geometric painter always tells us far more than we can see. A dead man lies on his bier wrapped in a shroud. The shroud is an enormous chessboard pattern above the corpse. The dead man himself 'is drawn so that both arms, both legs, triangular torso, and profile head are seen; in fact he is a standing man who has been revolved through ninety degrees and inserted in the space between the bottom of the shroud and the top of the bier; the painter feels the need to say that he had two arms, two legs, and a manly chest'. It would, I think, be justifiable to say that he felt that he was in some sense making a man (and not only a man but a hero) and that the visual impression of a man wrapped in a shroud would leave him without his essential parts. This conception of the artist as making rather than representing explains much in archaic art besides the actual conventions of representation. Statue or painted figure or vase address the spectator in the first person: 'Stop and pity Kroisos', or 'Timonidas painted me' [6]. The work of art is in some sense alive, and if it represents someone it is also his or her substitute.

Sappho appealed to 'Aphrodite of the painted throne' to help her, and her hearers in Lesbos would know which seated statue in what temple she meant. A caricature with a name on it could change the man named into its horrid likeness. The artist who could make such potent figures had more in common with the magician than with the photographer. He commonly from the late seventh century labelled his figures (and sometimes also animals and material objects); the name is in the nominative because he had in some sense made the person or thing, but late in our period artists began to use the genitive of the name instead of the nominative [7]. This is the beginning of the new conception of the artist's function: he ceased thereby to make men but started to 'imitate' them.

A glance at vase-painting from the end of the geometric period shows how the range of observation was increased. We have seen already how the human figure swelled out and became individualized by a wealth of inner markings; sometimes in the seventh century it was painted in flesh colour, although in the sixth century it was conventionalized again into black men and white women but with copious incision and added colour. Birds and animals underwent the same transformation and their kinds became more numerous, while plants and trees appear not infrequently [8].

In discussing portraiture we noticed how more and more observed detail was included within the conventional framework, until after our period the framework itself was abandoned for more realistic poses—in male figures ever-increasing elaboration of anatomy and in female figures the contrast between hair, eyes, cheeks and lips and between light and heavy dress materials. A wealth of observed detail can be found on sixth-century vases and two late examples may be quoted. One is an Attic hydria [9] in London with six women at a fountain house. The women all have their names and the fountain house is named Kallirhoe fountain. It has its portico and its lion-head spout gushing water into a hydria placed on a step; most of the women are walking away with a filled hydria upright on their heads; one is coming up with an empty hydria poised horizontally on a pad on her head. It is a pleasant picture of everyday Athenian life. The other picture is the Ionian Busiris hydria [10], which shows a remarkable knowledge of Egypt.

The painter knew that the King of Egypt wore an *uraeus* and a beardcase (hence his scrubby chin), that Egyptians were both light and dark-skinned, that they wore curious clothes with fringes and that negroes had thick lips and woolly hair. The spectator was expected to be interested in foreign peoples, an interest already shown in the Russian epic of Aristeas of Prokonnesos and to flower later in the geography of Hekataios and the history of Herodotos.

We are however particularly interested in the representation of the third dimension since this more than anything else restricts the painter to appearances. The full development of perspective and shading lies beyond our period, but there are a few details in which the painter already shows himself concerned with depth. Very early both vase-painters and sculptors were interested in clothing, vase-painters in its colours and elaborate patterns and sculptors also in its differences of texture. But until about the middle of the sixth century no real attempt was made to show its folds, but it lies quite flat on the body; from the middle of the century onwards sculptor and painter began to build up an elaborate system of folds which really gives some depth to the drapery[11]; a good early example is the Otago Dionysos with its careful zigzag folds emphasized by alternating black and red.

The chariot race and chariot drive were always exciting subjects, and presented problems of foreshortening and depth. The geometric painter was not content with the visual impression: he shows the two wheels side by side, he tips the floor up so that it can be seen, and paints both the chariot's side rails as well as its solid front. The horses' bodies may be amalgamated, but their foreparts, tails, and legs are shown distinctly. This is a chariot and horses with all its essentials visible. The seventh-century artist contented himself with a simple silhouette which shows a single horse and the chariot with one wheel and one rail. In early black-figure more depth was given by drawing the horses behind each other so that they overlapped, and sometimes they are also differentiated in colour. Soon after the middle of the sixth century an entirely new scheme was made to show the critical moment of rounding the turning post. On a black-figure vase by a painter associated with Exekias the chariot is drawn frontal; the riders remain in profile; the horses are drawn in profile but are moved across so that the chests and necks of all four are shown; the heads of the two centre horses are frontal [1] [2]. The scheme gives a tremendous impression of the torque required to turn the chariot and at the same time a considerable depth. The next step is to foreshorten the wheels and the body of the chariot; but this is inevitable when the initial step has been taken of representing depth and movement by violent contrasts of frontal and profile views. When he foreshortens body and wheels, the artist has abandoned 'creation' for 'imitation'.

The art of the archaic period shows not only a greatly extended range of observation but also this growing tendency to represent actual appearances rather than conventional views. In literature the beginning of this lively observation is to be found in the similes of the *Iliad* and the *Odyssey*, which can with some confidence be attributed to the last stage of the Homeric epic. It is probably true to say that the poets of the seventh and sixth century show more appreciation of visual and tactile values than Homer, but it must always be remembered how much in Homer is traditional and how closely attuned even the similes are to what they have to illustrate [1] [3]. From our point of view the extreme interest of the similes lies in their use to illustrate an unknown by a known: Homer finds in everyday life a number of known models to illustrate the heroic situation which he wants to make clear and convincing to his audience. After a long and on the whole successful day of battle Hektor orders a feast to be prepared and watchfires to be lit and promises victory in the morning. 'And they in great spirit sat all night upon the bridges of war and their many fires burned. As when in heaven the stars shine very clear about the shining moon and the upper air is still, and all the peaks and ridges and glades stand out, and the infinite sky is opened up to heaven. All the stars appear and the shepherd rejoices in his heart.' The poet starts from the multitudinous lights of the watchfires and that gives him his comparison with the stars, but he is more interested in conveying the peaceful confidence of the Trojans in general and Hektor in particular when a successful day is over, when any hostile raid will be detected in the light of the watchfires, and when victory is reasonably forecast for the next day. This peaceful confidence is like the confidence of the shepherd on a moonlit night, which not only presages a fine day and allows him to see that his flock is safe but also has its own peculiar soothing quality. The known experience of the shepherd is a kind of working model of Hektor's experience, which the poet wants his audience to understand.

Thales like any other educated Greek must have known his Homer and understood the value of the working model for conveying an understanding of the unknown. He said that the earth floated on water like a log and apparently used magnetic stone and amber to illustrate his conception that the material world was ensoulled [14]. The important point here is, I think, that, like Homer, he felt the need to make his conception of the unknown workings of the universe convincing by an appeal to everyday experience. We must distinguish the manner of presenting the theory from the theory itself. The manner of presentation is new and looks forwards to science. The views that the earth floats on water and that the material world is ensoulled are parts of a more comprehensive theory that all things arise from ensoulled water [15]. This view is essentially the same as Homer's view when he calls Ocean the origin of all things, but there is the important difference that Thales speaks of water and Homer speaks of Ocean. Thales' water may be ensoulled and therefore in some sense alive, if not divine, and capable of generating all things, but by calling it water he emphasizes that it is the ordinary everyday stuff that we drink. Homer's Ocean may be the source of all rivers, the boundary of the earth, and navigable in a ship, but he is also the father of Eurynome and the husband of Tethys, with whom he is quarrelling when Hera visits him. Homer's Ocean is an instance of the not uncommon unification in which the god and the natural phenomenon are identified. Homer used the divine name; Thales accepted the theory but uses the common name.

Homer's brief reference shows that the Greeks were interested in the origin of the world (or cosmogony) before Thales, and we have the further evidence of Hesiod and Alkman. These early Greek cosmogonies are themselves dependent on Oriental cosmogonies. Homer shows the closest affinity with the Akkadian creation epic and Hesiod with a Phoenician version. It has been argued that Thales drew directly on Eastern sources and there is general agreement on his knowledge of Babylonian astronomy and Egyptian land-measurement (geometry). But the brief reference in Homer implies that his contemporaries knew a creation poem and I see no necessity to suppose that Thales knew anything else; the question however is not of great importance. Nor does it matter for our purpose whether Homer and Hesiod themselves borrowed from the East or whether, as I rather suppose, the borrowing took place in the Mycenaean age[16]. The early Greek cosmogonies are important to us because they show us the kind of presuppositions with which Thales and his contemporaries started and the manner in which such statements were made.

Homer gives us three points. First, as we have said, the personal god is completely identified with the natural phenomenon. Secondly, Ocean is the origin of all things (*genesis* is a verbal noun, that from which all came into being) and Tethys is a mother: cosmogony is only thought of in terms of procreation. Thirdly, in another passage[17] Tartaros is as far below Hades as Heaven is from Earth; Homer demands a neatly symmetrical universe as a geometric artist would. Homer only refers briefly to these things, but Hesiod's *Theogony* is a full length poem, in which the theogony proper, the family tree of the gods, is preceded by a cosmogony. Hesiod begins by recounting his dedication on Mount Helikon: the Muses breathed into him divine speech that he might make known the past and the future[18]. This is therefore a prophet's revelation and not the argument of a philosopher. The result is a simple and intelligible arrangement in a family tree of all the things, physical, animate, and spiritual (including the Olympian gods) which surround man and baffle his comprehension. We are primarily concerned with the cosmogony[19].

First of all Chaos came into being, and then broad-breasted Earth, the sure seat of all, and Eros, who is the most beautiful among the immortal gods, loosener of limbs, and conquers the mind and careful wits in the breasts of all gods and men, and from Chaos Erebos and black Night came into being; and from Night Aither and Day came into being, whom she bore having conceived them by uniting with Erebos in love. And Earth first brought into being, equal with herself, starry Ouranos (heaven), that he might cover her completely, in order that there might be a sure seat for the blessed gods; and she brought into being the long Mountains, the lovely homes of the Nymphs, who dwell in the wooded mountains. She also bore the unharvested sea with raging waves, Pontos, without the passion of love. But from the bed of Ouranos she bore deep eddying Ocean and Koios and Krios and Hyperion and Iapetos and Theia and Rheia and Themis and Mnemosyne and Phoibe with her golden crown and lovely Tethys. After them her youngest came into being, crafty Kronos, most terrible of her children. And he hated his strong father.

The picture, which owes much to the Phoenician cosmogony, is clear enough—first an abyss, then Earth and Eros as a god of fertility; under the earth is Darkness (Erebos) and Night and over the earth the Upper Air (Aither) and Day. The Sky (Ouranos) completely covers the earth; between them are the long mountains and the sea. Then with the children of Ouranos and Earth Hesiod passes to theogony as distinct from cosmogony, and the hatred of the youngest child Kronos looks forward to the Eastern story of the succession of rulers leading up to the just ruler Zeus, who with his consort Themis and his daughters the Seasons guarantees the moral order of Hesiod's *polis* [20]. The verbs 'come into being', 'brought into being', 'bore' used in the cosmogony are the same as those used in the succeeding theogony; the cosmogony also is expressed in terms of procreation. The father is only named if Hesiod knew who he was; but the process is apparently the same whether there is a father or not. These beings are not only material like sea and mountains, but may be described by neuter nouns like Chaos (from which Erebos and Night come into being), Erebos (the father of Aither and Day), and the long Mountains; therefore the neuter word *hydor* used by Thales for water did not preclude its being a divine procreative force. If we read Hesiod's *Theogony* to the end, we must admit that equation in a family tree has some positive advantages: Chaos is the ultimate ancestor through Night of Death and Deception, Earth is the ultimate ancestor through Zeus and Themis of the Seasons, Justice, Good Order, and Peace: the moral order is thus based on the physical order, and this is made clear by the use of the family tree [21].

Alkman's cosmogony [22] is unfortunately only known from the fragmentary remarks of a learned but not very intelligent commentator. In this poem Alkman invoked the Muse to bless the girls' choir for which he was writing. He called the Muse daughter of Earth and Heaven; as elsewhere in Alkman the Muses are the daughters of Zeus, he may have brought in his cosmogony to explain their new parentage. The cosmogony is startling: Thetis made out of matter Poros (contriving) and Tekmar (end) and thirdly Skotos (darkness). Then she made Day and the Moon. Presumably Heaven and Earth follow soon afterwards. Alkman cannot have used the Aristotelian word *hyle* for matter: as he seems to interpret Thetis etymologically as 'the arranger', his word for matter may have been *pelos* (mud) with a pun on Peleus, Thetis' husband. What however is clear, is that Thetis operated as a craftsman and this is a conception which seems to be alien from early Greek cosmogonies, however natural it seems to us.

The poetic cosmogonies show us that the Greeks thought of the world arising by a process of generation from beings who could be considered either as materials or as persons and might either have masculine or feminine or neuter names: a neuter name did not preclude fatherhood or motherhood. We have also seen one instance of a symmetrical universe with the heaven as far above the earth as Tartarus is below it. The poets state and do not explain; Thales took two steps towards science and philosophy: he used comparisons from the everyday world to explain his ideas and he chose the impersonal water instead of the personal Ocean as the name for his original substance. We do not know that he constructed a geometrical universe, although he was a considerable mathematician who applied his knowledge of isosceles triangles to measuring the height of the pyramids and determining the distance of ships from land [23]. His successor Anaximander, however, shows this feeling for geometry in the proportions of his universe: the earth's depth is a third of its diameter, its diameter is a ninth of the circle of the fixed stars, and an eighteenth of the circle of the moon, and a twenty-seventh of the circle of the sun; the circular surface of the earth is divided into equal segments by the Mediterranean, Danube, Black Sea, and Nile, which are all joined to the surrounding Ocean [24].

Anaximander also explained how this geometrical universe arose and worked. The following is an attempt to reconstruct his explanation. His original element he called the 'boundless'. From it, whether by procreation or by separation, came the opposite substances (hot and cold, dry and wet) of our universe. The opposites 'pay reparation and satisfaction to each other for their injustice according to the ruling of time'. The earth is in the middle *like* the drum of a column. It is surrounded by air, which in its turn is surrounded by a sphere of fire *like* the bark on a tree. The surrounding fire was broken off and shut into rings of air to make the heavenly bodies. These rings are *like* chariot wheels with hollow rims; the rims are pierced at one point so that the fire pours out *like* the air from the nozzle of a bellows. The opening and shutting of the holes determines the phases of the moon and the eclipses of the sun and moon. Thunder and lightning are caused by the action of winds on clouds. The first men were nurtured inside fish-like creatures *like* viviparous sharks, and only came out when they were strong enough to look after themselves [25].

We have to reconstruct this picture from later accounts which are seldom verbatim quotations, and this accounts for its obscurity. Anaximander himself clearly made every effort to explain by comparison with everyday life. He thinks of seasonal changes, coast erosion and alluvial deposits, etc. as a balance of opposites which comes out even at the end of the year, and so compares it to payment exacted for theft in a law court. He uses trees, chariot-wheels, and bellows to explain his idea of the working of the heavenly bodies and the behaviour of sharks to illustrate what he believed happened to the earliest men. Even the traditional weapons of Zeus against the sinner, thunder and lightning, were now attributed to the behaviour of wind, and we can suppose that he (like his successor Anaximenes) had some model in ordinary experience to explain their action.

It is not so clear how he thought the whole process started, and our texts are to blame for this. We know however that the 'boundless' was 'immortal and indestructible and all-encompassing and all-steering and divine'. These are the titles of gods, and we must suppose that in some sense Anaximander's boundless gave birth to and controlled the Universe [26]. We can account for its name: Homer talks about the 'boundless sea'. In his terminology therefore Anaximander has taken a further step in depersonalization: Homer's personal Ocean became Thales' impersonal water; Thales' water has now become the boundless. Its only characteristic is that it has no bounds, whatever Anaximander meant by that: at least, I think it has two implications. First, Anaximander was conscious of its ancestry and meant his audience to remember the boundless sea, so that the boundless is something without limit or horizon. Secondly, it is contrasted with the finite elements which arise out of it. We cannot however say whether Anaximander spoke of them as the hot, the cold, the dry, the wet, or as fire, air, earth, water. But he certainly used the term 'the boundless' and so introduced into philosophy a kind of expression which was both useful and dangerous, the general noun formed by the neuter adjective with the definite article.

In Mycenaean Greek adjectives were already used as nouns, but what later became the definite article was still a demonstrative pronoun. The masculine adjective 'three-footed' is used for a tripod cauldron; the feminine adjective 'of horses' is used for a chariot; the neuter adjectives 'of the people' and 'of roses' are used for public land and rose-oil [27]. It is the use of the neuter which is particularly interesting. Homer speaks of 'stripping all round *the black* of the oak' in making a fence; 'the black' is the heart, and the article is used with the adjective to contrast it with the unexpressed lighter part of the wood. In Anaximander's own time Sappho spoke of 'the bright and the beautiful of the Sun'. This kind of phrase seems to have originated with material things like public land and rose-oil, and I think that it is still material in Sappho—*not* the brightness of the sun but the bright stuff in the sun [28]. Similarly Anaximander's boundless is a material substance of which a particular quality is emphasized. If, like his successors, he also spoke of the 'hot' and 'the cold', they would similarly be material substances imbued with this quality, and they are so used by Anaxagoras in the fifth century. They are also used by the doctors, who extend the use from physical constituents of the body to mental constituents of the soul; they speak as easily of the 'the brave', 'the industrious', 'the fierce' or 'the idle' as they speak of 'the hot' or 'the cold' [29]. This is one of the dangers inherent in this mode of expression: 'the hot' in the body does correspond to some discoverable physical fact; 'the brave' is a much less useful way of stating that a man may be expected to perform actions which will classify him as brave. The other danger is the vagueness of such expressions: 'the good' may mean a member of the class of good things or all the members of the class or the perfect member of the class. Even the perfect member of a class is still a member of the class. It will therefore be spoken of in terms applicable to a thing rather than to a quality. Therefore when Plato speaks of 'the good itself', although he means the quality of goodness, he still says that it is good, in spite of the logical fallacy involved in speaking of a quality possessing the quality which it itself denotes [30].

I have digressed to discuss the further history of this kind of expression, which leads to some of the most puzzling passages in Plato's dialogues. I must now return to Anaximander's successor, Anaximenes. I suggested, when discussing the rise of individualism in the sixth century, that the meaning of *psyche* had changed somewhat between Thales and Anaximenes; Thales' water was ensoulled (*empsychon*) because it had life and could produce life, Anaximenes gave the *psyche* not only life and life-giving power but the power of control. It seems possible that Anaximenes may have felt that Anaximander's Boundless was satisfactory as a reservoir of stuff from which worlds could arise, but did not have of itself the power of steering which was attributed to it. *Psyche* was now credited with the power of control; but *psyche* was traditionally breath or a component of breath, and breath was air. Air breathed out may be hot or cold, thin or thick. Anaximenes combined the properties of soul with the properties of breath and found in air a basic substance which could both make the necessary changes and possessed the necessary driving forces. This air is god and the origin of gods and of all things that exist: so far the old language of the poetic cosmogonies persists [31]. The new world picture has to provide for floating on air and is explained by comparisons. The sun is flat *like* a leaf; the earth is *like* a table; the stars are *like* nails set in crystal; the stars (and presumably the sun) revolve round the earth *just as* the felt is wound round our heads. As Anaximenes explained the setting of the sun by its disappearance behind high mountains, this last comparison must, I think, be to a turban made of a long strip of felt; a man can see the felt when he winds it round his forehead but not when it passes behind his head. Anaximenes accepted Anaximander's explanation that thunder and lightning were caused by the pressure of the wind on clouds, but compared the flash of lightning to the foam struck up by the oar in the dark sea [32].

In these last two comparisons Anaximenes has advanced beyond Anaximander. He has moved from illustration to working model. The movement of the band round behind the head is a working model of the assumed movement of the heavenly bodies, and the pressure of the hard oar on the dark, wet sea is a working model of the pressure of the compact air on the dark, wet cloud. An explanation of this kind which (like the developed Homeric simile) touches the thing to be explained at a number of points is much more convincing than the illustration which only touches it at a single point. Anaximenes' two other working models mark a further step forward [33]. The first is the passage already discussed in which he spoke of breath and air containing the whole universe just as our *psyche* controls us. The second is his explanation of the process by which air becomes other things. This is not (or not only) generation but rarefaction and densification: 'When breath is compressed by the lips, it becomes cold; when it falls out of loose lips, it becomes hot.' By an extension of both processes the thin air could become fire and the compressed air water and earth. Both these statements are of great importance in themselves; the first initiates the long series of comparisons between the macrocosm of the world and the microcosm of man; the second gives a purely physical explanation of the process by which the world came into being in its present form and an eminently sensible explanation. Both are working models in the sense described, but they differ from the other working models in that they employ the actual material of the unknown to be explained. For Anaximenes air (soul) does contain and control the human body, and human breath does grow cold when compressed and hot when relaxed. The working model uses the same material in the same way as the unknown original. It may therefore be regarded not only as a working model but as the germ of an inductive argument. The terminology was not invented until much later, but perhaps we may see in Anaximenes the beginning of a demand for a closer relation between illustration and original and, therefore, for stricter control of arguments.

However much they owed to poetic cosmogonies, the three philosophers of Miletos tried to explain the world in terms of everyday life. Their claim to have originated science and philosophy rests on their assumption that the world can be explained in such terms. The great problem that they left was how to make such explanations cogent, how to substitute for brilliant guesses, which were backed by a minimum of at most plausible observation, arguments which could be accepted as highly probable, if not necessary. The three men whose youth still falls in our period, Pythagoras, Xenophanes, and Herakleitos, were less interested in the physical constitution of the universe than their predecessors but made important contributions to the technique of argument. We have said something already about their place in the history of individualism as the successors of Anaximenes [3 4], and their main interest might perhaps be defined as wisdom, the wisdom of the ascetic life with its hope of immortality for Pythagoras, the wisdom of an all-powerful God for Xenophanes, and the wisdom that can be apprehended in the universe for Herakleitos. This puritan view of the world which looks forward to the plays of Aeschylus and the sculptures of the temple of Zeus at Olympia does not concern us here, but we must glance briefly at Pythagoras as a mathematician and at the kinds of argument used by Xenophanes and Herakleitos.

The chronology of the men themselves and of their writings is difficult to establish and both Pythagoras and Xenophanes probably lived the most important part of their lives in S. Italy; but as they are both mentioned as learned (but not wise) men by Herakleitos, some of their works must have been known in Ionia (whether written there or not) well before the end of the sixth century, and as Xenophanes mentions Pythagoras (as we have seen), Pythagoras was probably the oldest of the three. He is also the most difficult to apprehend, since we only know him from later reports and it is extremely hard to distinguish what is his from what was added by his followers and successors. We must however believe that he discovered that the chief musical intervals are expressible in simple numerical ratios between the first four integers, that he invented the theorem which bears his name, and that he believed in some sense that things were numbers. This last belief undoubtedly gave rise to all kinds of nonsense but also to the very fruitful idea of seeking for a numerical relationship between things. The musical scale had yielded brilliantly to a numerical interpretation, and one kind of right-angled triangle has sides which can be expressed as 3, 4, 5. Thus, quite apart from his influence in other ways, his success may have encouraged others both to look for proportions in the universe and to cast their arguments into the form of proportions [35].

Precedents can be found for both procedures earlier, but they seem to have gained a fresh impetus in the late sixth century. Homer's Phoenix warns Achilles to tame his mighty wrath, because even the gods, whose valour, strength, and position is greater, allow themselves to be swayed by prayers [36]. This is a proportional argument: man's flexibility should be as much greater than god's as man's strength is less. Xenophanes [37] uses the same kind of argument the other way round to establish his god, who is greatest among gods and men, in no way like mortals in structure or in thought; the whole of him sees, appreciates, and hears; he remains in the same place and without toil makes all things vibrate by the power of his mind. We have only fragments of the argument, but the other term which we have lost would surely have been the wise king as the most successful mortal. Expressed as a proportion, the argument is that, as mortality is to immortality, so is the effectiveness of mortal wisdom to the effectiveness of divine wisdom. It is, of course, also a quite different application of the argument from the microcosm to the macrocosm, which Anaximenes started.

Before considering Xenophanes' inductive arguments let us glance at the further development of arguments from proportions. Professor Hermann Fränkel has shown that a considerable number of fragments of Herakleitos can be reduced to a proportional pattern of the form $A : B = B : C$. A simple example is: 'man is called fool by god, as child is by man'. God is as far above mature man in intelligence as mature man is above a child. The difference between this type of statement and an ordinary comparison is that here the relationship of the unknown (the intelligence of god) to the first known (the intelligence of man) is fixed by its equation with the relationship between the first known and the second known (the intelligence of a child). Fränkel has suggested that Herakleitos had perhaps learned from the Pythagoreans about the harmonious contrasts in a succession of tones with equal intervals and about correspondent progressions in geometry and algebra. At any rate for Herakleitos proportions were not only a form of argument

and a truth of mathematics but a phenomenon to be apprehended in the universe, which is 'everliving fire kindling in
measures and being extinguished in measures' [38]. If we look on
to the end of the fifth century and, still further, into the fourth
century, we find that proportional arguments are common in
the early Hippocratic treatises and in Plato. In the *Gorgias*
Plato himself stresses the connection of this form of argument
with geometry: 'I want to say like the geometers that as cos-
metics is to gymnastic, so is sophistic to law-giving, and as
cooking is to medicine, so is rhetoric to justice.' This is a four-
term proportion which Plato uses to discover the nature of
rhetoric and clinches by another four-term proportion which
establishes the nature of sophistry. He makes a very large use of
proportions in other dialogues, notably the successive and
interconnected proportions of the Sun, the Line, and the Cave
in the *Republic*. It is, as Aristotle sees, a useful method of
defining a relationship AB and CD when A and C are not
species of the same genus. Except in mathematics, where an
exact quantitative relationship exists between the terms, it is
not so much a form of argument as a useful shape for precise
statement [39].

The other interesting arguments in Xenophanes may be
classed under two headings, induction and experiment. Anaximenes' argument from the behaviour of human breath and
human soul is the germ of an induction. Xenophanes has two
interesting inductive arguments. He saw (or heard of) shells
inland and in the mountains, fossil fish and seaweed in the
quarries of Syracuse, fossil laurel in Paros, and flat shapes of all
sea things in Malta. He argued from this to a previous (and a
future) wet state of the earth. This is a theory based on a considerable number of widely spaced observations and can reasonably be called an induction. Similarly Xenophanes uses three
pieces of evidence to establish the general rule that man makes
god in his own image. 'The Ethiopians say that their gods are
snub-nosed and black, and the Thracians say theirs are blue-
eyed and red-haired.' Thirdly, 'Homer and Hesiod attributed to
the gods all the faults that bring reproach among men, theft,
adultery, and deceiving each other'; Homer and Hesiod, to
whom evidently the Greeks of Xenophanes' time, like Herodotos, attributed their knowledge of the gods, made the gods in

man's errant likeness. Thus the general truth is established by two pieces of evidence from foreign sources and one piece of evidence from the most authoritative Greek sources⁴⁰.

So far he has used inductive argument, but he then proceeds: 'if oxen and horses and lions had hands or could paint and sculpt like men, horses would paint the gods' forms like horses and oxen like oxen, and each would sculpt their bodies like their own.' It may seem far fetched to call this an experiment, but it is in fact an invitation to test the general rule on any kind of subject and an assurance that it will prove to be true. This is the form in which experiments are normally given by fifth-century writers, who do not report the performance of an experiment but invite their readers to undertake it and tell them the result. Thus Anaxagoras, wanting to show that our senses cannot distinguish between a pure substance and a mixed substance, says: 'if we take two colours, black and white, then pour drop by drop from one to the other, our vision will not be able to distinguish small changes.' This is an experiment in the modern sense of 'forcing nature to answer the precise questions which we ourselves decide will help us to solve a problem', and experiments are phrased in the same form in the early Hippocratic treatises⁴¹.

I have suggested that proportional argument was probably borrowed by Herakleitos from the mathematicians. Two other kinds of argument, which we first find in the early fifth-century philosopher Parmenides, seem to have been transferred from mathematics to philosophy. One is the deductive argument by which Parmenides establishes the properties of Being from its definition; this kind of argument is used in any kind of geometrical proof which deduces a solution from existing propositions; and if we can accept, as is generally agreed, that the early Pythagoreans proved that the three angles of a triangle equal two right angles by deducing the new proposition from two known propositions, this kind of mathematical proof antedates Parmenides⁴². The other kind of argument is the *reductio ad absurdum*: Parmenides accepts his opponent's position and then proceeds to show that it leads into absurdities. This kind of argument is so common in later mathematics that it seems to me much more likely that the philosophers borrowed it from the mathematicians than vice versa⁴³. Parmenides was not (or not only) a pupil of Xenophanes but had a Pythagorean teacher, and it is among the Pythagoreans that a transference of mathematical argumentation to non-mathematical subjects might have been expected.

The mathematical proof has universal validity; it is what the Greeks call 'necessary' (*anankaion*). This is its great attraction for the philosopher. Long ago Hesiod's Muses had said 'we can tell many lies like the truth', and Xenophanes perhaps echoed the phraseology when he said 'let these be our opinions as resembling the truth'. Xenophanes hints at two words, *doxa* (opinion) and *eikos* (resembling, probable), which have a long subsequent history in epistemological questions. This fragment is presumably the conclusion of an argument which possibly began: 'the clear no man knows, nor will anyone know, either about the gods or about all that I say about everything. For even if one were in fact for the most part to say what was perfect, yet he himself does not know it, but opining is ordained for all [44].' Knowledge and truth belong to the gods; man has only opinion. How can he ensure that his opinion resembles the truth? His own mental capacity is, of course, one factor in the problem, and Herakleitos, who also saw the difficulty, had no doubt of his powers. But Herakleitos, although he expresses himself more like a prophet than a teacher, gave his own arguments, as we have seen, a quasi-mathematical form.

It was a great step forward to recognize the problem and to invent a terminology for it. Ideally 'proof' and 'necessity' would only be used of mathematical argument, and 'probability' and 'signs' of all argument from the seen (the observable phenomena of this world) to the unseen, which for the Greeks included the unobservable parts of the human body and the unexplored parts of the world, as well as what we should call spiritual or metaphysical realities [45]. In practice, of course, the excitement of discovery may lead the discoverer to claim too much: Herodotos, in his discussion of the Nile, says that it is not *probable* that it flows from snow, but when he has assembled his four 'testimonies' (that the country from which the Nile flows has (1) hot winds, (2) no rain or ice, (3) black inhabitants, and (4) hibernating birds), he concludes that if there were any snow in this country, 'none of these things would be, as *neces-*

sity proves.' But the great popularity of the word *probable* and the distinction which came to be drawn between signs sometimes and signs always indicating a particular unseen cause, show the appreciation of the need to control arguments. In the three main classes of argument based on comparisons, the working model, the experiment, and the induction, the control may be called quantitative: the induction must be based on as many instances as possible, and the working model and the experiment must have the maximum possible number of cross references to the original. But when general truths have been established by these means and made as cogent as possible, they may then be used as the premises in a mathematical argument, which within its own limits has the certainty of proof[46].

Thus the mathematical arguments provide a framework within which the general truths established by observation or otherwise can be related to each other. I think it is possible that the mathematicians influenced the philosophers in two other ways. Mathematical terminology is both convenient and precise. I should like to suggest that the sophists who belonged to the generation after Parmenides were preoccupied with formal grammar and the precise meanings of words partly because they were trying to give the terms of a philosophical argument the same sort of precision as the terms of a mathematical proof[47]. Precision of this kind is probably impossible to achieve, although it is probably also desirable that the demand for it should ever and again be made and receive some sort of satisfaction. Convenience however can be achieved although not without a dangerous sacrifice of precision. The philosopher and the scientist observe this brave man or that sick man, but they need to discuss 'valour', which is common to all brave actions, or 'jaundice', which is the label for all sick men of a particular kind. They need a terminology as remote from individual actions or sufferings as the mathematician's sphere is from his son's football. We have seen that one way which the Greeks found for making such convenient general terminology was to use the neuter of the adjective with the definite article, and that this use was dangerous both because of the extremely wide range of reference and because even in its most abstract uses 'the good' somehow preserved the flavour of a concrete good thing. Curiously enough a very similar danger besets the other most convenient general term, the feminine abstract noun.

These became both numerous and frequent in the technical literature of the fifth century. 'When they do not reveal these things and nature herself makes no discharge of her own accord, medicine has discovered constraints by which nature may be forced without harm to herself to make discharges [48].' This picture of harmless torture to establish the truth is a concise and persuasive statement of the theory of experimental medicine: if the patient does not visibly reveal his symptoms, doctors who are skilled in experimental procedure can cause him to make revealing discharges without doing himself any harm. Medicine is a shorthand for doctors who can use a particular technique efficiently. Nature is a shorthand for all sick bodies. Because they are both feminine, they can be spoken of as persons: nature is unwilling but can be constrained, medicine has discovered means of constraining. They are put together as interrogator and prisoner, just as Hesiod puts Justice, Good Order, and Peace together as daughters of Zeus. Nature is both all sick bodies and the prisoner in the interrogation, just as Homer's Ocean is both navigable water and a god quarrelling with his wife. It is perfectly true that personified Ocean was presumably much more real in Homer's time than three hundred years later when the Hippocratic text was written, but the tradition of personifying and worshipping abstracts was still alive in the fifth and fourth century. The danger, of which we have spoken, is that these feminine abstracts may seem to be goddesses, just as the neuter abstracts may seem to be things, and may so be given a kind of reality which does not belong to abstracts. The danger is only too apparent in Plato's theory of Ideas [49].

The attempt to show, however partially and sketchily, this one aspect of Greek scientific thought, the assumption from which they started, the types of argument they used, the cross-fertilization of one branch of thought by another, the demand for controls, and the development of terminology, has led us far beyond the boundary of our period. It must always be remembered how fragmentary our sources are for the sixth century. In particular we have lost all early mathematical texts, which might have clarified the debt of Xenophanes and Herakleitos. Yet we know enough to say that the decisive step was taken in our period even if fruition was only much later and then only partial. The decisive step was the abandonment of the mythical cosmogony for a world that arose from water. However much of the old view survived with the new, this step was decisive for several reasons. The first reason is the basic assumption, however restricted and dimly apprehended, that the world should be explained by the interaction of material causes. The second reason is that it entailed also rational explanation instead of apocalyptic statement. Thales started from the practical world of politics and commerce, and if he himself did not write a book his successor Anaximander wrote in prose. Later philosophers might use poetry or poetical prose but they always argued as well as prophesying. Explanation presupposes an audience and must be intelligible to the audience; a third reason therefore why this step was decisive was that the explanation was by comparison with things that the audience knew and could check, or, to put it another way, the theory was based on verifiable observation. An audience worthy of explanation is a critical audience, and a critical audience demands controls. The decisive step entailed, therefore, the growth of controls: that observations would be verified, that they must be both relevant and sufficient to support the theory, that the arguments themselves should be orderly and valid. Thus the whole later development is foreshadowed in the work of the three great Milesians whose lives cover the last century of our period.

The attitude of the Milesians encouraged detailed observation, and in this respect the geographers and the doctors are their successors—also the artists, who show more and more concern with the details of external appearance. Anaximander, at least, demanded further that the universe should not only be intelligible but formally beautiful with its simple proportions: the boundless gives rise to a world which is geometrically finite. This Greek love for clear and precise pattern can be traced back to Homer and geometric art (and far beyond). There pattern dominates, but we must always remember the realistic detail of the Homeric similes and the Geometric potters' readiness to turn the knob of a lid into a horse or bird. The painters, sculptors, and poets of the seventh and early sixth century were in revolt against formalism, and vital individualism showed itself in many different ways—in the swagger of Archilochos, the great stormy figures of proto-Attic vases, the tremendous imagery of Solon, the Gorgon of Corfu, the widely different ecstasies of maenads and fat men. Well before the middle of the sixth century, however, the control of pattern had reasserted itself (and it is here that Anaximander belongs) and dominated sculpture, painting, and poetry—the *peplos kore* and her successors, Exekias and the Amasis painter, the lyrics of Ibykos and Anakreon, and, as we must suppose, the drama of Thespis and his immediate successors—until Aeschylus, Pindar, and the Olympia sculptors led a new revolt already prepared in different ways by Anaximenes, Pythagoras, Xenophanes, and Herakleitos. To realize and to formalize are the essential driving forces of Greek art, poetry, and thought. Both are always present, though in varying degrees. Sappho's passionate songs have their own beautifully conceived shape, Exekias' carefully balanced composition reveals the tragedy of Ajax' suicide, and the stormy swaggering Archilochos[50] expresses the classical philosophy of moderation:

> Heart with clueless cares confounded,
> Up and fight your foe, breast forward,
> Standing firmly as you wait him;
> If you win, no blatant triumph,
> Nor beaten lie at home lamenting;
> Sober be your joys and sorrows.
> Know the ebb and flow of men.

THE BEGINNINGS OF
PHILOSOPHY AND SCIENCE

(References to works of art will be found under the appropriate numbers
in the list of monuments at the end.)

1. The chronology is difficult in detail, but the order is certain. I assume
that Thales lived approximately 624-548; Anaximander 610-540;
Anaximenes 585-520; Pythagoras 570-500?; Xenophanes 570-475;
Herakleitos 544-484. The evidence is quoted and discussed by K. R.,
pp. 74, 100, 143, 217, 163, 182. H. Thesleff, *Soc. Sc. Fennica Comm.
hum. litt.* 23 (1957), 3 f., argues interestingly for dating Xenophanes
about thirty years later. A pointer may however be given by Bowra's
observation that his poem against athletes, which also implies that
his wisdom is already formed, does not mention the race in armour
which was first held in 520 (cf. above Ch. II, n. 63). The reference to
Thracians and Ethiopians (cf. below n. 40) would perhaps mean more
to East Greeks than West Greeks, Herakleitos' (K.R. 193 = *VS.* B 40)
knowledge of Pythagoras and Xenophanes is more likely to derive
from work written in the East than work written in the West. This
all seems to me to fit rather better with the traditional dating of
Xenophanes, although I see the attraction of making him an early
classical rather than a ripe archaic author.

2. Particularly F. M. Cornford in the posthumous *Principium Sapientiae*:
U. Hölscher, *Hermes*, 81 (1953), 385; and most recently W. K. C.
Guthrie, *In the Beginning*, 14 f.

3. References for Thales above Ch. I n. 50. Thales in politics, Hdt. 1,
170 (K.R. 64).

4. *Athenian Art and Literature in the fourth century*, 82 f., pl. 12; A.
Rumpf, *J.H.S.*, 67 (1947), 10 ff., excellently sketches the development
of painting from the late fifth century.

5. Athens, N. M. 990, *M.H.*, 204, fig. 22; cf. also *C.Q.* 33 (1939), 175 f.

6. Kroisos: no. 7, fig. 8. Cf. above Ch. II n. 84. Timonidas: no. 72. Cf.
also above II n. 68b. Other instances are given *C.Q.* 33 (1939), 177.
Cf. also the dedications of Mantiklos (no. 1), Nikandre (no. 19), Cheramyes (no. 22). The archaic inscription is normally a speech made by
the sculptured or painted figure or by the vase or other monument.

7. Sappho, cf. above Ch. II, n. 53. Caricature: I believe that this is the
meaning of Pliny's story about Boupalos and Athenis, who exhibited
a portrait of Hipponax to laughing crowds (*N.H.* 36, 12); cf. also
Hipponax 45 D. Objects and animals labelled: e.g. Attic François
vase, no. 46, in the Troilos scene fountain house, hydria, seat, and in
the wedding scene altar; Laconian Arkesilas cup, no. 85, weighbeam
and scales; Corinthian Andromeda amphora, no. 80, monster and
donkeys. Names in the genitive: *C.Q.*, 33 (1939), 169.

8. On portraiture in sculpture and painting, cf. above Ch. II, n. 70-84. Animals, birds, and plants in post-geometric vase-painting, e.g. Attic Analatos hydria, no. 31; Sophilos' wedding, no. 45; Burgon group ploughing scene, no. 49; Amasis painter indoor scene, no. 61; Corinthian Chigi jug hare-hunt, no. 67; Timonidas' bottle, no. 72; Parian deer, no. 88, fig. 2; Caeretan hydria, Apollo and Hermes, no. 96. Many others could be quoted as a glance through any picture book will show: in particular, I have not mentioned the whole large class of East Greek vases decorated with friezes of animals, particularly wild-goats, e.g. Lane, *Greek Pottery*, figs. 16-18.

9. London, British Museum, B 331 (manner of Lysippides painter); *A.B.V.* 261/141.

10. No. 101. Aristeas, cf. above Ch. II, n. 14.

11. Colours and patterns in drapery on early vases: e.g. Attic Analatos hydria, no. 31; Melian Apollo and Artemis, no. 89, fig. 4; Corinthian Amphiaraos krater, no. 83; Attic François vase, no. 46. Differences of texture in sculptured drapery: e.g. goddess from Auxerre, no. 9, fig. 5; Hera of Cheramyes, no. 22 (cf. above I, n. 48). The history of the treatment of folds in sculpture can be seen very clearly on the seated figures from Branchidai, Miletos, in F.N. Pryce, *Catalogue of Sculpture in the British Museum*, I, pt. 1. Of the works mentioned above the Hera of Cheramyes, no. 22, in spite of the differentiated texture has completely flat drapery, as has the Kore of Anaximander, no. 23; Chares from Branchidai, no. 26, slightly after the middle of the century, has a plastic rendering both of the folds of the chiton and of the edge of the himation where it falls between the legs; this treatment is slightly more advanced in the seated Aeakes from Samos, no. 27, of about 540 and much more still in the later statues from Branchidai. On Attic black-figure vases the first beginning of folds can be seen on Sophilos' wedding, no. 45, the hanging cloak of Chariklo; Dionysos in Lydos' return of Hephaistos, no. 52, has simple angular folds at the bottom of his himation; Exekias paints shallow systems of rounded folds; the woman's chiton in the Amasis painter's 'lyre player', no. 61, has quite an elaborate stacking of rounded folds; the Dunedin Dionysos by the Antimenes painter, no. 62, looks forward to the more elaborately piled curved folds of the last quarter of the century.

12. The chariot in geometric painting: e.g. Athens, N.M. 990, with references given above n. 5. A good early seventh-century example is the Analatos painter's krater, no. 32. Subsequent development is admirably treated by J. White, *Perspective in Ancient Drawing and Painting*, Hellenic Society, Supplementary Paper, no. 7, 10 f. Overlapping of horses in black-figure painting: e.g. chariot-race of François vase, no. 46, and on reverse of Corinthian Amphiaraos krater, no. 83. Note that shortly after the middle of the seventh century the line of warriors on the Chigi jug, no. 67, overlap each other, and on the early sixth century metope of the Sikyonian treasury at Delphi, no. 14, the cattle overlap, just like the horses in contemporary chariot

races. Black-figure vase with chariot turning, no. 57, fig. 13. The later development is discussed by J. White, loc. cit.

13. M. Treu, in *Von Homer zur Lyrik*, has recently studied and, I think, overemphasized the difference between Homer and the lyric poems in appreciating sensible and tactile values. In general, however, it is true that, partly because they bulk large in relation to the rest of the poem, descriptions of nature in the lyric poets seem to have a new warmth, colour, richness and importance; particularly Alkman 58 D (über allen Gipfeln), 94 D (the *kerylos*); Sappho 2 L-P (the precinct of Aphrodite); Ibykos 6 D (the garden of the Nymphs). On the subject matter of Homeric similes see *M.H.*, 220 f.; on their function see *M.H.*, 224 f. The simile quoted is *Iliad* 8, 553 f. Cf. Adam Parry, *T.A.P.A.*, 87 (1956), 1 f.

14. The log: K.R. 86 (*VS.* A 14). Magnetic stone and amber: K.R. 92 (*VS.*, A 1). The whole conception is much easier to understand if it is remembered that the boundary between thing and person was not so clearly drawn (or was not drawn in the same place) by the early Greeks as by ourselves. So in Homer 'iron itself draws a man on' (*Od.* 16, 294), Sisyphos' stone is 'shameless' (*Od.* 11, 598), spears are 'yearning to taste flesh' (*Il.* 11, 574), and this kind of personification survives in the technical terminology of scientists and doctors (cf. *J.W.C.I.*, 17 (1954), 15 f.). We have noticed already that not only the sculpted or painted figure but also the vase itself may speak in the first person (cf. above n. 6), and the vase may be made more obviously alive by being given eyes, nose, and ears; this practice is very old but dies out (except for the special case of moulded head vases) before the end of the sixth century (cf. *C.Q.* 33 (1939), 178).

15. Thales: K.R. 87, 93, 95 (*VS.* A 12, 22, 23). Homer: *Il.* 14, 200-210 (Hera's visit to Ocean, boundary of earth, origin of gods, and husband of Tethys); 14, 245 (origin of all); 21, 195 (origin of rivers); 18, 399 (father of Eurynome); *Od.* 10, 508 (navigable water). The identification of god and natural phenomenon is closely akin to the kind of personification described in the preceding note. Other such identifications in Homer are the Sun, the Winds, the Earth, Fire, etc., The Winds had a priestess in Mycenaean Knossos, and in Mycenaean Pylos Demeter seems to have been both a goddess and a measure of arable land (cf. *Coll. Latomus*, 28 (1957), 531); in the early sixth century Solon still can say (24, 4 D): 'greatest mother of the Olympian gods, black Earth, whose boundary stones I took up'.

16. On the Oriental sources of the Creation myth and the possibility that the Greeks had already borrowed them in Mycenaean times, see *M.H.* 84 ff. (and in more detail *Minos*, 4 (1956), 109 ff.). Cf. also K.R., discussion on nos. 4-6. Thales and Babylonian astronomy: K.R. 76-8. Thales and Egyptian land-measurement: K.R. 68-71.

17. *Il.* 8, 13-16.

18. Cf. above Ch. II, n. 8.

19. Hesiod, *Theogony*, 116-38, quoted and discussed K.R. 24. I have omitted ll. 118-19, both of which are omitted also in some early quota-

tions of the passage: 118 is harmless but restricts the 'all' of 117 to 'the gods who dwell on Olympos'; 119 puts Tartaros on a level with Earth and Eros. Tartaros is not used in the subsequent genealogy, and in the next generation its place is taken by Erebos, which becomes the husband of Night.

20. On the Phoenician source see U. Hölscher, *Hermes*, 81 (1953), 393 ff.; he finds there both Chaos and Eros, who has no further part in Hesiod except in so far as he was the procreative force. Eros would not be strange to Hesiod's Boeotian audience, as the 'unwrought stone', which survived at Thespiai till Pausanias' time (9, 27, 1) alongside statues of Eros by Praxiteles and Lysippos, must have been very old; its worship presumably ensured the fertility of crops and animals as well as women. Ocean and Tethys, it will be observed, come quite late in this theogony after the cosmogony is over but still belong to the generation before Zeus. Of this generation Hyperion, Theia, and Themis have been found on the Mycenaean tablets and may be pre-Greek divinities with Greek names, whose great age has been remembered. The succession myth—Ouranos dethroned by Kronos and Kronos by Zeus—has Phoenician, Hittite/Hurrian, and Akkadian parallels: cf. above n. 16, and particularly F. M. Cornford, *Principium Sapientiae*, 191 f.; A. Lesky, *Anz. Wien. Ak.*, 1950, 148; U. Hölscher, loc. cit.

21. Zeus, Themis, and the Seasons with their new Hesiodic names show how useful personification and genealogy are for stating the relation between abstract concepts (or even natural phenomena). In Homer the war-god Ares has a sister Strife (*Il.* 4, 440) and a son Panic (*Il.* 13, 299); Panic and Fear are his grooms (*Il.* 15, 119), and Panic has a companion Flight (*Il.* 9, 1). In Alkman Success is the sister of Good Order and Persuasion and the daughter of Forethought (44 D), and Dew is the daughter of Zeus and the Moon (43 D). In Ibykos (8 D) the beautiful Euryalos is child of the Graces, darling of the Muses, nursed by Aphrodite and Peitho (cf. above, Ch. I, n. 46). When Hesiod called the Seasons Justice etc. (probably also when he made them daughters of Zeus and Themis) he was giving new names and a new genealogy to an existing group: so also satyrs, maenads, nymphs, fat men are existing groups which can be given names to suit the particular moment—the fat men on the Corinthian vase (no. 78) already quoted (Ch. I, n. 43) are called Reveller, Sportive, Backbender, Sidebender, Pleasurelover. (The names of satyrs and maenads have been collected by C. Fränkel, *Satyr und Bakchennamen auf Vasenbildern*.) The writer of the Homeric epigram to the potters thought of some such figures as plaguing the potters if they did not pay him and gave them names connected with mishaps to pottery such as breaking, bursting, overfiring, bad kneading of the clay, and damage before firing (R. M. Cook, *C.R.* 62 (1948), 55 on *Vita Herodotea*, 445-8). Cf. also below n. 49.

22. *Ox. Pap.* 24, 2390 fr. 2. The Muses are daughters of Zeus in frs. 40, 67, 68 D. Mimnermos also made them daughters of Earth and

Heaven; both poets had connections with Lydia, and it is possible
that we should look to Lydia and beyond to the old Phoenician poem
for some of the details of Alkman's strange cosmogony. There Mot =
mud came very early in the cosmogony, and the sun and moon shone
forth from Mot (Hölscher, *Hermes*, 81 (1953), 394). The commentator
is confused and uses Aristotelian terminology, but the succession
(Matter), Thetis, Poros, Tekmor is certain. In the long Partheneion
fragment (1D) Alkman calls Aisa and Poros the oldest of the gods,
and the ancient commentator on that passage equates Poros with
Hesiod's Chaos, but that may be only his guess; if Alkman there had
this cosmogony in mind, he equated Aisa (fate) with his new Thetis.
Our commentator quotes 'and third Darkness' both after Tekmor
and after 'Day and moon', but he says clearly that darkness preceded the lights, and therefore I think that Alkman must have made
Poros, Tekmor, and Darkness his trio. The craftsman conception
is otherwise only found in the Pandora story (and it is arguable that
Pandora was originally an earth goddess) and in the very strange
sixth-century cosmogony of Pherekydes of Syros in which Zeus
weaves a cloak for Chthonie and embroiders in it Earth and Ocean
and the houses of Ocean (K.R. 54 = *VS*. B 2). I have disregarded all
cosmogonies of this type (they are discussed in the first chapter of
K.R. and by Jaeger, *Theology of the early Greek philosophers*, 61 f.),
because no line seems to lead from them to the scientists.

23. Thales' mathematics, K.R. 81-2 (=*VS*. 1, 20, 21). Cf. K. von Fritz,
    Archiv für Begriffsgeschichte, I, 77.

24. Anaximander's geometrical universe: cf. above Ch. I, n. 50. K.R.
    124, 127-9 = *VS*. A 10, 11, 21-2. His map of the circular surface of
    the earth: K.R. 96, 100-2 = *VS*. 1, 6. K.R. 102 (=Hdt. 4, 36),
    Herodotos' scornful mention of a map which gives a perfectly circular
    earth surrounded by Ocean, does not mention Anaximander but is
    plausibly referred to him. The Black Sea was well known to Milesians
    by Anaximander's time, and he is himself said to have led a colony to
    Apollonia near the mouth of the Danube (colonization of the Black
    Sea had been going on since the late eighth century). It seems to me
    likely that he made the Danube and the Nile the other two divisions
    of the land masses; Herodotos himself still says that the two rivers
    have 'equal measures' (2, 33) which implies symmetry. On early Greek
    maps see J. O. Thomson, *History of Ancient Geography*, 97 f.; J. L.
    Myres, *Herodotus, father of history*, 34 f.

25. Cf. in general W. K. C. Guthrie, *In the beginning*, 31 ff., 48. 'The
    boundless': K.R. 110 (=*VS*. A 15). The opposites: K.R. 120-3
    (=*VS*. A 9-10). The view taken of the process depends on whether
    stress is laid on 'productive' in K.R. 123 or on 'separating out' or 'off'
    in K.R. 120-21. Guthrie, *H.T.R.* 45 (1952), 90 and Cornford, *Princi-
    pium Sapientiae*, 163, 180 stress the former; K.R. the latter. If Anaxi-
    mander used 'separating off', the image may have been the Homeric
    champion emerging from the throng for single combat (*Il.* 5, 12).
    'Reparation etc.': K.R. 112 (=*VS*. B 1); this is verbatim quotation

of Anaximander. 'The drum': K.R. 124 (= *VS*. B 5). 'The bark': K.R. 123 (= *VS*., A 10). 'Chariot-wheels etc.': K.R. 127-8 (= *VS*., A 21-2). Our sources are not consistent here, and it is likely that Anaximander used several images without building them into a working model. I have assumed that the wheels must revolve round us and we must see the fire spouting from holes in their inner rims. It is difficult to combine this with the picture of a wheel with its hub full of fire, which runs through the spokes to the rim (*VS*., A 21). The trumpet and the bellows may be alternative images for the actual emission of the fire. 'Thunder and lightning': K.R. 132 (= *VS*. A 23). 'Sharks': K.R. 140 (= *VS*. A 30).

26. 'The boundless': K.R. 110 (= *VS*. A 15). 'The boundless sea', *Il*. 1, 350; Ocean, on the other hand, is 'the bounds of the earth', *Il*. 14, 200. On the terminology, cf. R. B. Onians, *Origins of European thought*, 310 ff.

27. See M. Ventris and J. Chadwick, *Documents in Mycenaean Greek*, 87 on demonstratives; 385 f. (vocabulary) for references to discussions of *ti-ri-po* (tripod), *i-qi-ja* (chariot), *da-mi-jo* (people's land), *wo-do-we* (rose-oil). Cf. also *e-re-mo* 'uncultivated land', *a-ki-ti-to* 'unsettled land' etc.

28. *Od*. 14, 12. Monro, *H.G.*, para. 260e, and Chantraine, *Grammaire Homérique*, II, 163, explain the use of the article as due to the implied contrast: the contrast is expressed in *Il*. 1, 106-7 'the good (singular) . . . the bad (plural)'. Sappho 58 L-P (=65 D): this appears to me the most probable explanation of this difficult line.

29. Anaxagoras K.R. 496 (= *VS*. B 4). Hippocrates, *de aeribus etc.*, 24. In the Anaxagoras passage 'the hot' and 'the cold' are used collectively for all matter imbued with heat. In the Hippocratic passage 'the fierce' etc., is an undefined amount of the 'fierce element' possessed by certain people. Cf. my article in *Acta Congressus Madvigiani*, II, 32, and P. Chantraine, *ibid.*, V, 20 f.

30. Cf. G. Vlastos, *Philosophical Review*, 63 (1954), 324 ff. Cf. also below, n. 49.

31. Cf. above Ch. II, n. 62, and in general Guthrie, *In the Beginning*, 48 f. 'Air as god etc.': K.R. 147-9, 144 (= *VS*. A 10, 7).

32. 'leaf' and 'nails': K.R. 157-8 (= *VS*. A 14). 'table': K.R. 153 (= *VS*. A 20). 'felt': K.R. 159 (= *VS*. A 7); the explanation of K.R. and others that the felt is a hemispherical cap which revolves round the head is unsatisfactory; why should it revolve? B. Farrington's suggestion of a stone in a sling is very attractive but there seems to be no evidence that 'felt' can mean this (*Proc. Royal Institution*, 23 May 1945). The turban is, I think, the pointed headgear worn by dancers on contemporary Chiote vases (e.g. *J.H.S.* 44 (1924), pl. 11) and the 'wasped covering' of Anakreon's Artemon (54 D, the material, not the shape, is ridiculed). 'The foam of the oar': K.R. 161 (= *VS*. A 17).

33. Control of *psyche*: K.R. 163 (= *VS*. B 2); cf. above Ch. II, n. 62. Rarefaction etc.: K.R. 146 (= *VS*. B 1). On forms of argument in the Pre-socratics see O. Regenbogen, *Quellen und Studien*, B 1, 1931,

187 f.; H. Diller, *Hermes*, 67 (1932), 31 f.; B. Snell, *Discovery of the Mind*, 213 f.; and my article in *Acta Congressus Madvigiani*, II, 33 f.

34. Cf. above Ch. II, n. 63-5.
35. On the chronology, see above n. 1. On Pythagoras, see K.R. p. 229 ff.; J. S. Morrison, *C.Q.* 6 (1956), 135 f., particularly 152 ff.; K. von Fritz, *Archiv für Begriffsgeschichte*, 1, 79 ff.
36. *Il.* 9, 496 f.
37. Xenophanes, K. R. 173, 175, 174 (= *VS*. B 23, 24, 26, 25), Cf. below n. 44.
38. Fränkel, *W.F.*, 253 f., paitic. 265 (Pythagoreans). The example quoted is *VS*. B 79; very similar in form is K.R. 215 (= *VS*. B. 53): god is to man, as free man is to slave. G. S. Kirk (*The Cosmic fragments*, 78) agrees that this proportional form of exposition was dear to Herakleitos but finds that Fränkel includes too many fragments under this heading. Kirk gives also the interesting example of Herakleitos' proportional calculation of the Great Year (op. cit., 300 f. on *VS*. B 100, A 13, 19). The idea of proportion in the universe (which Anaximander had expressed as payment for injustice) is found in the fragment quoted, K.R. 220 (= *VS*. B 30), and in K.R. 221 (= *VS*. B 31), where it is expressed as *logos*.
39. The author of *Ancient Medicine* ends his account of the discovery of medicine (13) with a proportion: 'the diet of sick men stands in the same relation to the diet of healthy men as the diet of healthy men to the diet of animals,' and the four-term proportion is very common in the treatises discussed by Regenbogen, op. cit., n. 33; cf. also P. Grenet, *L'Analogie dans Platon*, 253. On the proportional argument in Plato cf. P. M. Schuhl, *Fabulation Platonicienne*, 41 ff. The instances quoted are *Gorgias* 465b, *Rep.* 506, 509, 514; cf. also *Phaedo* 109b. The example which Aristotle gives in the Ethics (1096b 28) 'sight in the body equals intuition in the soul' is itself a reminiscence of Plato's Line; later he defines it as 'an equality of proportions in at least four terms' (1131a 31). For other applications cf. *Post. Analytics*, 76a 39, 98a 20.
40. Xenophanes' fossils etc.: K.R. 187 (= *VS*. A 33). Man makes god in his own image: K.R. 170 (= *VS*. B 14). Ethiopians etc.: K.R. 171 (= *VS*. B 16). Homer and Hesiod: K.R. 169 (= *VS*. B 11). The authority of Homer: *VS*. B 10.
41. Xenophanes' experiment: K.R. 172 (= *VS*. B 15). Anaxagoras: K.R. 536 (= *VS*. B 21, which gives the full text of Sextus; he seems to have preserved the form and substance, if not the actual words of Anaxagoras). Anaxagoras also used bladders (wineskins) and pipettes (*klepsydra*) to prove that air was corporeal; this must have been an experiment but we only know the fact, not the form (K.R. 498 = *VS*. A. 68-9). The *klepsydra* in Empedokles (K.R. 453 = *VS*. B 100) is not used experimentally but is a working model to illustrate the nature of breathing as conceived by Empedokles. Experiments can be found in the Hippocratic treatises (e.g. *de morbo sacro* 14; *de aeribus etc.* 8, 57) and one of the most interesting is the experiment to

show the growth of the human embryo: a hen is made to sit on 20 eggs and the content of one is examined each day (*Corpus Hippocraticum*, Littré, 530/10, cf. Regenbogen, op. cit., n. 33). In the *Art* 13 the principle of experiment in medicine is stated: 'medicine has discovered constraints in which nature may be forced without harm to herself to make discharges,' and an example is given: if the quality of sweat is to be examined, the man can be made to sweat by running.

42. Parmenides, K.R. 347, 1-4, 16-21; 350-2 (*VS*. B 8). Pythagorean geometry: Heath, *Manual of Greek mathematics*, 121 f.; Von Fritz, quoted above n. 35. Parmenides and Pythagoras, K.R. 339-40 (= *VS*. A 1; 12). This kind of mathematical deductive argument is further developed by Plato in his use of *hypothesis* and *diairesis*.

43. Parmenides' *reductio* K.R. 347, 5-15 (*VS*. B 8). The method is the backbone of Zeno's paradoxes and Mr. Lee (*Zeno of Elea*, 112) thinks the geometers may have got it from him but the reverse seems to me much more likely. Melissos uses this form of argument to defeat the pluralists who uphold the existence of sensibles (K.R. 392 = *VS*. B 8): if the many things exist and our senses report them correctly (this is his opponents' argument which he for the moment accepts), they must exist in the Parmenidean sense of permanence, etc.; but our senses report continual change, and this is incompatible with permanence; therefore his opponents' position is absurd. The statement that our senses report continual change is established by a number of instances, i.e. by an inductive argument. This use of inductive arguments within the framework of the *reductio* is the common form of the Socratic *elenchos* in the early Platonic dialogues, e.g. *Rep*. I, 335a.

44. Hesiod, above Ch. II, n. 8. Xenophanes: the terminology of K.R. 190 (= *VS*. B 35) echoes K.R. 189 (= *VS*. B 34), and may therefore end a section of argument which began with K.R. 189. K.R. offer two translations for the last phrase of 189: 'seeming is wrought over all things' or 'fancy is wrought in the case of all men'. The verb should be taken in its Homeric sense: 'is ordained' (e.g. *Il*. 18, 120). I see no way of choosing between 'all things' and 'all men', unless the use of the preposition suggests 'things' as 'men' would be in the simple dative. For *dokos* K.R.'s 'seeming' and 'fancy' (cf. D's *Scheinmeinen*) are less good than Untersteiner's *congetturare* (*Senofane*, ccxix ff.). But Untersteiner takes the fragment as a contrast between X. knowledge and other people's fancies. K.R. follow Sextus, to whom we owe the fragment, in taking it as a contrast between divine knowledge and human opinion, which in fact is the basis of Xenophanes' view of god, cf. above n. 37. Xenophanes (cf. Ch. II, n. 63) had, of course, no more doubt of his own powers than Herakleitos (K.R. 193 = *VS*. B 40). But neither would claim to be more than the best human interpreter of sense-data, and the interpretation is performed by human powers and can be appreciated, if they take the trouble, by other human beings: this, I think, is implied by Herakleitos (K.R. 197, 198, 201 = *VS*. B 1, 2, 107), and when he says (K.R. 247 = *VS*. B 93) 'the

lord whose shrine is at Delphi neither speaks nor conceals but gives a
sign', he means that human interpretation is possible.

45. The three important words are *semeion*, *tekmerion*, and *eikos* (with
their cognate verbs). Herakleitos in the fragment just quoted (n. 44)
uses the verb which comes from the same root as *semeion*: 'gives a
sign'. His perhaps slightly younger contemporary Alkmaion of
Kroton uses the verb connected with *tekmerion* (K.R. 285 = *VS*. B 1):
'the gods have clarity about unseen things as about mortal things; we,
as men, can only use tokens'; not much later *tekmeria* is coupled with
martyria ('testimonies', used in a geographical argument by Herodotos,
see next note) by Athena in Aeschylus' *Eumenides* (485), and *tekmerion* is used of Orestes' footprints in the *Choephori* (205). Both words
are used by philosophers, historians, doctors, and orators in the
sense of pieces of evidence and of arguments based on pieces of
evidence (or indeed of deductive arguments). Much later Aristotle
(*Prior Analytics* 70b 1-6; *Rhet*. 1357a 34-b 25) distinguished the
two, advocating the use of *tekmerion* for a sure symptom (he is ill
because he has fever) and *semeion* for an unsure symptom (he has
fever because he breathes fast).

In the same passage of the *Rhetoric* Aristotle distinguishes *eikos*
(probable) from *anankaion* (necessary), as that which happens for
the most part among things which could happen otherwise. It was
commonly so used in the fifth century, and Thucydides calls Themi-
stocles the best *eikastes* (forecaster) of what was actually going to
happen in the future (1, 138, 3, cf. A. Rivier, *Un emploi archaïque de
l'analogie*, 41 f.). But it had also a specialized application to pre-
dictability on the basis of character: it is already so found in Aeschylus (*Eum*. 194) and is common in the fifth century, e.g. *De aeribus etc*.
22, 47; Hdt. 1, 42, 1; Thuc. 1, 4, 1; it was ruthlessly exploited by the
orators in lawcourt cases, and Aristotle's examples of probability in
the *Prior Analytics* (70a 2) are of this kind: the envious hate and
those beloved feel affection (I think this is the correct translation in
spite of Philoponos).

The general principle that what we can see is a clue to the understanding of what we cannot see is stated for their different purposes
by Anaxagoras (K.R. 537 = *VS*. B 21a), the doctors (*Ancient Medicine*, 22; *Diet*, 1, 11; *Art*, 10 f.), Herodotos (2, 33).

46. Hdt. 2, 22, 2. Aristotle (*Prior Analytics*, 68b 27) says that only
enumeration of all the instances can make induction a conclusive
argument. The doctor who invented the experiment with the hens
(above n. 41) had some idea of the need for controlling experiments.
Empedokles' descriptions of his two working models—the pipette
for breathing (K.R. 453 = *VS*. B 100, cf. D. J. Furley, *J.H.S*. 77 (1957),
31) and the lantern for sight (*VS*. B 84)—are very carefully written
to show all possible cross references between model and original: the
technique is still further worked out by Plato in his use of *paradeigma*
in the technical sense: e.g. *Politicus* 277 where the rules are given,
followed by an examination of the art of weaving (279) as a *paradeig-*

ma for the kingly art (287), cf. V. Goldschmidt, *Le Paradigme dans la dialectique Platonicienne*. On inductive arguments within the framework of a mathematical argument, cf. above n. 43.

47. e.g. Protagoras, *VS*. A 1, grammatical terms; 26, correct use of words; Prodikos, *VS*. A 13-19, distinction of synonyms.

48. Hippocrates, *Art*, 13. Cf. the rather similar personification of medicine by Plato in *Gorgias* 501a, cf. also 464c, 518a.

49. Homer cf. above n. 15. Hesiod and his successors cf. above n. 21. On the growth in the number and use of abstract nouns it may be observed that one type, the nouns (like *physis* 'nature') which are formed by attaching *-sis* to the stem of a verb, shows ten times as many examples in Plato as in Homer, and that they occur forty times as frequently in the early Hippocratic writings as in Homer. (On these nouns cf. now R. Browning, *Philologus*, 102 (1958), 60; P. Chantraine, *Acta Congressus Madvigiani*, V, 15.) *Pheme* (rumour) was given an altar in Athens in 465 and *Eirene* (peace) in 371 (cf. Nilsson, *Eranos*, 50 (1952), 31 ff.). An Attic vase painter of the late fifth century puts *Hygieia* (health) among the Hesperids when Herakles visits them, and the maenads surrounding Dionysos on Attic vases of the same time are named after the concomitants or conditions of Dionysiac worship Peace, Brightness, Good Cheer, and Longing. Plato seems to be thinking of Herakles' drive to Heaven and his sojourn in the garden of the Hesperids, when he pictures the charioteer of the human soul catching glimpses of Justice herself, Knowledge herself, and Modesty herself in their place beyond heaven (*Phaedrus* 248, cf. *Art and Literature in fourth-century Athens*, 40 f.; *J.W.C.I.*, 17 (1954), 14 f.). Even in passages which are not mythical or persuasive (e.g. Vice as a runner, *Ap.* 39b; Pleasure as a Fury, *Phaed.* 83d) the Ideas have objective reality, and *either* they approximate to goddesses (feminine abstracts), when they are called patterns and sensibles are called copies, imitating them, or reaching out for them, *or* they approximate to things (neuter abstracts, cf. above n. 30), when they are in sensibles or sensibles partake of them, cf. Ross, *Plato's Theory of Ideas*, 228.

50. Archilochos 67a D.

List of Monuments
Discussed in the Text

The monuments are arranged under A. Sculpture (including reliefs, bronzes, terracottas), B. Painting. Within these headings they are grouped chronologically under areas of origin, 1. Attica and Boeotia, 2. Crete and Peloponnese, 3. Cyclades, 4. Asia Minor including Rhodes, Chios and Samos, 5. Italy and Sicily.

The order in each complete entry is number, references to pages and figures in this book, description of object, subject, date, provenance (where provenance is given in brackets, this means place of origin as distinct from place of discovery, if these are different), museum, and modern literature (recent discussions, standard works, and accessible illustrations).

A. SCULPTURE

1. ATTICA AND BOEOTIA

1. (Ch. I n. 21, 33; II n. 82; IV n. 6)
   Bronze statuette, Apollo. 700/675. From Thebes. Boston Fine Arts Museum.
   Ref: *A.J.A.*, 39 (1935), 511; Lamb, *Greek Bronzes*, 74, pl. 20c; Picard 136, fig. 35; Karo 70; Hoekstra, *Mnem.*, 10 (1957), 222.

2. (Ch. II n. 83, fig. 7)
   Marble statue, naked male. 600 *c*. From Sounion. Athens, N.M. 2720.
   Ref: Richter, *Kouroi*, no. 2; Lippold, pl. 10/1; Karo 250.

3. (Ch. II n. 83)
   Marble statue, naked male. 600 *c*. From Attica. New York 32.11.1.
   Ref: Richter, *Kouroi*, no. 1; *Archaic*, fig. 10-11; Philadelpheus, *B.S.A.*, 36 (1936), 1.

4. (Ch. I n. 24)
   Terracotta relief, Achilles and Amazons. 600 *c*. From Attica. New York 42.11.33.
   Ref: Richter, fig. 9; von Bothmer, *Amazons*, no. 3.

5. (Ch. II n. 81)
   Marble statue, draped female. 570/60. From Attica. Berlin.
   Ref: Richter, fig. 90-1; Lippold, pl. 10/2; Rumpf, *Critica d'Arte*, 14 (1938), 47.

6. (Ch. II n. 81)
   Marble statue, draped female. 540 *c*. From Athens. Athens, Acr. 679.
   Ref: *A.M.S.* 18; Richter, fig. 123-4; Lippold, pl. 23/2.

7. (Ch. II n. 84; IV n. 6; fig. 8)
   Marble statue, naked male (Kroisos). 540/30. From Anavysos. Athens. N.M. 3851.
   Ref: Philadelpheus, *B.S.A.*, 36 (1936), 1; Richter, fig. 113-14; *Kouroi*, no. 114; Peek, no. 1224.

2. PELOPONNESE AND CRETE

8. (Ch. III n. 28)
Terracotta masks, Gorgons. 700 c. From Tiryns. Nauplion 4506-8.
Ref: Hampe, *Sagenbilder*, 63, pl. 42; Karo, 32 ff.; Webster, *W.S.*,
69 (1956), 108.

9. (Ch. I n. 16, 18; II n. 53, 81; IV n. 11; fig. 5)
Limestone statue, draped female. 640/30. From (Crete). Paris,
Louvre 3098, from Auxerre.
Ref: Jenkins, *Dedalica*, 42; Rumpf, *Bonner Jb.*, 135 (1930), 78;
Lippold, pl. 2/3.

10. (Ch. III n. 17)
Bronze statuettes, dancing goatmen. 625/600. From Arcadia. Athens,
N.M. 13.788.
Ref: Lamb, *Greek Bronzes*, 42; Brommer, *R.E.*, s.v. Pan, 953.

11. (Ch. I n. 45)
Bronze shieldband, birth of Athena. 625/600. From (Argos). Olympia.
Ref: Kunze, *Olympische Forschungen*, II, 79, Beil. 6.

12. (Ch. II n. 81)
Limestone statues, Kleobis and Biton. 600/580. From (Argos).
Delphi.
Ref: Poulsen, *Delphi*, 90; Tod, *G.H.I.*, no. 3; Karo, 106; Richter,
fig. 32; *Kouroi*, no. 11; Lippold, pl. 5/1.

13. (Ch. I n. 28)
Limestone pediment, Gorgon (with Pegasos and Chrysaor) and
panthers; death of Priam; Zeus and giant. 600/580. From (Corinth).
Corfu.
Ref: Payne, *NC.*, 240; Rodenwaldt, *Korkyra*; Karo, 113 f.; Richter,
fig. 20-23; Lippold, pl. 6/1, 7/1.

14. (Ch. I n. 28; IV n. 12)
Limestone metopes, Europa; Kalydonian boar; Argonauts; cattle
raid. 580/70. From (Sikyon). Delphi.
Ref: Poulsen, *Delphi*, 86; Karo, 133 f.; Richter, fig. 148; Lippold,
pl. 4/1.

15. (Ch. I n. 24)
Bronze shieldband, Adrastos, Amphiaraos, and Lykourgos. 575/50.
From (Argos). Olympia.
Ref: Kunze, *Ol. Forsch.*, II, 175, Beil. 15.

16. (Ch. I n. 44)
Bronze shieldband, Ajax and Aristodamos. 575/50. From (Argos).
Olympia.
Ref: Kunze, *Ol. Forsch.*, II, 150.

17. (Ch. I n. 44)
Bronze shieldband, Theseus and Peirithoos. 575/50. From (Argos).
Olympia.
Ref: Kunze, *Ol. Forsch.*, II, 112.

18. (Ch. I n. 40; III n. 28)
Terracotta masks, Gorgons. 560/40. From Sparta. Sparta.
Ref: R. M. Dawkins, *Artemis Orthia*, pl. 49/2, 69/1; Pickard-Cambridge, *Dithyramb etc.*, figs. 19-25; *G.T.P.*, no. F 21; *W.S.* 69 (1956), 108.

3. CYCLADES

19. (Ch. II n. 81; IV n. 6)
Marble statue, draped female dedicated to Artemis by Nikandre. 660/50. From Delos (Naxos). Athens, N.M. 1.
Ref: Jenkins, *Dedalica*, 68; Picard, 570; Richter, fig. 42; Lippold, pl. 11/2; Karo, 92; *M.H.* 210; Geffcken, *Griechische Epigramme*, no. 31.

4. ASIA MINOR

20. (Ch. III n. 17)
Moulded vase, phallic daimon. 700/675. From Samos. Samos.
Ref: *G.T.P.*, no. F 23.

21. (Ch. III n. 17)
Bronze statuette, goat-headed phallic man. 600/550? From Samos. Athens, N.M. 6091.

22. (Ch. I n. 48; II n. 81; IV n. 6, 11)
Marble statue, draped female dedicated to Hera by Cheramyes. 570/60. From Samos. Paris, Louvre 686.
Ref: Buschor, *Altsamischer Standbilder*, II, 25; Karo, 201; Richter, fig. 165; Lippold, pl. 14/1.

23. (Ch. I n. 49; IV n. 11)
Marble statue, draped female dedicated by Anaximander. 560 *c.* From Miletos. Berlin 1599.
Ref: Lippold 47; Darsow, *J.d.I.*, 69 (1954), 101 f.

24. (Ch. II n. 68, 81)
Marble statue, winged victory, possibly by Archermos. 550 *c.* From Delos (Chios). Athens, N.M. 21.
Ref: Picard, 366; Rumpf, *Critica d'Arte*, 14 (1938), 47; Karo, 221; Richter, fig. 186, 190; Lippold, pl. 7/4; Geffcken, *Griechische Epigramme*, no. 29.

25. (Ch. I n. 47; II n. 81; fig. 6)
Marble head, female, from column drum of Artemis temple. 550 *c.* From Ephesos. London, British Museum B 91.
Ref: Richter, fig. 182-3.

26. (Ch. I n. 49; IV n. 11)
Marble statue, Chares seated. 550/40. From Miletos. London, British Museum B 278.
Ref: Karo, 211; Richter, fig. 177.

27. (Ch. I n. 49; IV n. 11)
Marble statue, seated male or female dedicated to Hera by Aiakes. 540 *c.* From Samos. Samos.
Ref: Buschor, *Altsamische Standbilder*, II, 40; Tod, *G.H.I.*, no. 7; Richter, fig. 261; Lippold, pl. 13/4.

28. (Ch. III n. 13)
Terracotta mask, satyr. 525 *c*. From Samos. London, British Museum 523.
Ref: *G.T.P.*, no. F 26; *W.S.*, 69 (1956), 108.

5. ITALY AND SICILY

29. (Ch. I n. 28)
Sandstone metopes, mythical scenes. 600/570. From Paestum. Paestum.
Ref: Zancani-Montuoro and Zanotti-Bianco, *Heraion alla Foce da Sele*, II, 1954; Richter, fig. 204-6.

B. PAINTING

1. ATTIC

30. (Ch. I n. 24)
Proto-Attic amphora, man carrying cloak; lion; chariots. 710/680. New York, 21.88.18.
Ref: J. M. Cook, *B.S.A.*, 35 (1935), 184, pl. 50.

31. (Ch. II n. 70; IV n. 8, 11)
Proto-Attic hydria (Analatos painter), dance; lions; deer. 710/680. From Analatos. Athens, N.M. 313.
Ref: Cook, op. cit., 166, pl. 38b, 39; Pfuhl, fig. 79.

32. (Ch. IV n. 12)
Proto-Attic krater (Analatos painter), chariots; lions. 710/680. Munich 1351.
Ref: Cook, op. cit., 173, pl. 41; Pfuhl, fig. 84; Rumpf, pl. 3/8.

33. (Ch. I n. 23; III n. 28)
Proto-Attic amphora (Polyphemos painter), Odysseus and Polyphemos; lion and boar; Perseus and Gorgons. 680/50. From Eleusis. Eleusis.
Ref: *J.H.S.*, 74 (1954), Suppl. 30; Mylonas, *Praktika*, 30 (1955), 29; *A.J.A.*, 62 (1958), 225.

34. (Ch. I n. 27)
Proto-Attic stand (Polyphemos painter), Menelaos and Greek chiefs. 680/50. From Aegina. Berlin A 42.
Ref: Cook, op. cit., 189; S. P. Karouzou, *A.E.*, 1952, 160; Rumpf, pl. 4/1; Mylonas, loc. cit.

35. (Ch. I n. 24, 38; II n. 71; III n. 17)
Proto-Attic krater (Ram jug painter), Lichas and captives (?); Apollo and Artemis; proto-satyrs, smooth and hairy. 680/50. From Aegina. Berlin A 32.
Ref: Karouzou, loc. cit.; Rumpf, pl. 3/10; *D.B.F.*, pl. 3; *G.T.P.*, no. F 1.

36. (Ch. I n. 24; II n. 71)
Proto-Attic krater (Ram jug painter), chariots; Antenor and Trojan chiefs. 680/50. From Athens. Athens, Acropolis 368.
Ref: Karouzou, op. cit., 162, fig. 24-5; Beazley, *P.B.A.*, 43 (1957), 243.

37. (Ch. I n. 23; II n. 71)
Proto-Attic oenochoe (Ram jug painter), Odysseus' escape from
Polyphemos. 680/50. From Aegina. Aegina.
Ref: Cook, op. cit., 187, pl. 53; Karouzou, op. cit., Rumpf, pl. 4/3.

38. (Ch. I n. 24)
Proto-Attic amphora, Argonaut wrestlers; chariot. 650/30. From
Kynosarges. Athens, N.M.
Ref: Cook, op. cit., 196, pl. 56-8; *D.B.F.*, 12.

39. (Ch. I n. 24, 53)
Black-figure skyphos-krater (Chimaera painter), Chimaira and
Pegasos. 625/600. From Athens. Athens, Ceramicus 154.
Ref: *A.B.V.* 3/3; *M.H.*, 179, 211.

40. (Ch. I n. 53; II n. 73)
Bf. neck-amphora (Nettos painter), Herakles and Nessos; Gorgons.
625/600. From Athens. Athens, N.M. 1002.
Ref: *A.B.V.* 4/1; *D.B.F.*, pl. 5/1; Pfuhl, fig. 85, 89; Richter, fig. 85, 89;
Richter, fig. 1, 4.

41. (Ch. I n. 24, 53)
Bf. krater (Nettos painter), Perseus; Harpies. 625/600. From Aegina.
Berlin 1682.
Ref: *A.B.V.* 5/4; *D.B.F.*, pl. 5/2; Richter, fig. 2.

42. (Ch. I n. 24, 53)
Bf. skyphos-krater (Nettos painter), Prometheus freed. 625/600.
From Vari. Athens, N.M. 16384.
Ref: *A.B.V.* 6; *B.C.H.* 1939, pl. 51/1.

43. (Ch. III n. 15, 26)
Bf. tripod kothon (KY painter), Komos: padded men and women.
600/575. Athens, N.M. 12688.
Ref: *A.B.V.* 33/1, 680; Payne, *NC.*, 196, fig. 88a.

44. (Ch. I n. 24)
Bf. dinos (Sophilos), funeral games of Patroklos. 600/575. From
Pharsalos. Athens, N.M. 15499.
Ref: *A.B.V.* 39/16; Rumpf, pl. 9/3; Richter, fig. 108.

45. (Ch. I n. 17; IV n. 8, 11)
Bf. dinos (Sophilos), wedding of Peleus and Thetis attended by
Nysai. 600/575. From Athens. Athens, Acr. 587.
Ref: *A.B.V.* 39/15; Pf., fig. 202.

46. (Ch. I n. 17, 26, 35; III n. 20, 31; IV n. 7, 11, 12)
Bf. volute-krater (Kleitias), mythological scenes. 570 *c*. From Chiusi.
Florence 4209.
Ref: *A.B.V.* 76/1; *D.B.F.*, pl. 11; Lane, pl. 36; Pfuhl, fig. 215, 217;
Richter, fig. 107.

47. (Ch. I n. 35, 36, 43)
Bf. hydria (Kleitias), Nereids. 570 *c*. From Athens. Athens, Acr. 594.
Ref: *A.B.V.* 77/8; *D.B.F.*, pl. 12, 1-2; Rumpf, pl. 9/9.

48. (Ch. III n. 15, 20)
    Bf. amphora of Panathenaic shape (Burgon group), Return of
    Hephaistos. 570/50. Oxford 1920. 107.
    Ref: *A.B.V.* 89/2; *C.V.*, pl. 4/1; 9/2.

49. (Ch. I n. 35; IV n. 8)
    Bf. cup (Burgon group), dance before Demeter; ploughing. 570/50.
    From Camiros. London, British Museum, 1906. 12-15.1.
    Ref: *A.B.V.* 90/7; Lane, pl. 38b; Ashmole, *J.H.S.*, 66 (1946), 8.

50. (Ch. I n. 36)
    Bf. neck-amphora (Camtar painter), Herakles and Amazons. 570/50.
    From Vulci. Cambridge 44.
    Ref: *A.B.V.* 84/2; *C.V.*, pl. 8/2 and 9/3; von Bothmer, *Amazons*,
    pl. 2/2.

51. (Ch. I n. 36)
    Bf. neck-amphora (Timiades painter), Herakles and Amazons. 570/50.
    From Vulci. Boston 98. 916.
    Ref: *A.B.V.* 98/46; von Bothmer, *Amazons*, pl. 5.

52. (Ch. III n. 15, 20; IV n. 11)
    Bf. column-krater (Lydos), Return of Hephaistos. 560/40. From
    Sicily. New York 31.11.11.
    Ref: *A.B.V.* 108/5; Rumpf, *Sakonides*, pl. 21-3.

53. (Ch. III n. 11, 26)
    Bf. cup (Heidelberg painter), dancers in costume. 560/40. From
    Greece. Amsterdam 3356.
    Ref: *A.B.V.* 66/57; *G.T.P.*, no. F 3.

54. (Ch. III n. 12)
    Bf. cup, satyr and fat-man on phallos pole. 560/40. From Italy.
    Florence 3897.
    Ref: *G.T.P.*, no. F 2.

55. (Ch. III n. 26, 44; fig. 12)
    Bf. pyxis, youths dressed as maenads. 560/40. From Eleusis. Eleusis
    1212.
    Ref: *G.T.P.*, no. F 4.

56. (Ch. III n. 24)
    Bf. amphora (painter of Berlin 1686), chorus of 'Knights'. 560/40.
    From Cervetri. Berlin 1697.
    Ref: *A.B.V.* 297/17; *G.T.P.*, no. F 5.

57. (Ch. IV n. 12; fig. 13)
    Bf. amphora (Group E), Herakles and Geryon; chariot wheeling.
    550/40. From Vulci. London, British Museum B 194.
    Ref: *A.B.V.* 136/56; White, *Perspective* (H.S. Suppl. 7), pl. 1c.

58. (Ch. I n. 35; II n. 76)
    Bf. amphora (near Exekias), victorious athlete. 550/30. Boulogne.
    Ref: *A.B.V.* 149/2; *B.S.A.*, 32 (1932), pl. 1.

59. (Ch. II n. 75; III n. 38; fig. 10)
    Bf. amphora (Exekias), suicide of Ajax. 550/30. Boulogne 558.
    Ref: *A.B.V.* 145/18; Pf. 234; Rumpf, 12/11; *D.B.F.*, pl. 32/1.

60. (Ch. III n. 25)
   Bf. amphora (Swing painter), chorus of 'Giants'. 560/40. Christchurch, University of Canterbury, Logie Collection.
61. (Ch. II n. 76; IV n. 8, 11)
   Oenochoe (Amasis painter), victorious lyre-player at home. 550/30. From Vulci. Vatican 432.
   Ref: *A.B.V.* 151/48; *J.H.S.*, 51 (1931), pl. 9; Karouzou, *Amasis painter*, 24, pl. 41.
62. (Ch. IV n. 11.)
   Bf. neck-amphora (Antimenes painter), Dionysos with maenads and satyrs. 540/20. Dunedin 48.231.
   Ref: *A.B.V.* 272/88; Anderson, pl. 5.
63. (Ch. II n. 76; fig. 14)
   Bf. pelike (manner of Acheloos painter), Gigantomachy; rhapsode with audience. ?510. Dunedin 48.226.
   Ref: *A.B.V.* 386/12; Anderson, pl. 6.

2. PELOPONNESE AND EUBOEA

64. (Ch. I n. 24)
   Proto-Corinthian aryballos (Ajax painter), Zeus and Typhon. 680 *c*. From Corinth. Boston 95.12.
   Ref: Payne, *Protokorinthische Vasenmalerei*, pl. 11; Dunbabin and Robertson, *B.S.A.*, 48 (1953), 176; cf. Lorimer, *B.S.A.*, 37 (1937), 178.
65. (Ch. I n. 24; III n. 17)
   Proto-Corinthian kyathos (Boston painter), Orpheus singing (?), satyr. 675/60. From Ithaca. Ithaca 52.
   Ref: Robertson, *B.S.A.*, 43 (1948), 21, 58; Dunbabin and Robertson, op. cit., 178; Webster, *R.B.*, 36 (1954), 581 f.
66. (Ch. I n. 23; II n. 71; fig. 3)
   Argive krater, Odysseus and Polyphemos. 675/50. From Argos. Argos.
   Ref: Courbin, *B.C.H.*, 79 (1955), 1; Dunbabin (1957), pl. 4/1.
67. (Ch. I n. 27; II n. 76; IV n. 8, 12)
   Proto-Corinthian olpe (Macmillan painter), hoplites; lion-hunt; judgement of Paris. 650/40. From Veii. Rome, Villa Giulia.
   Ref: Payne, *NC.* no. 39; Dunbabin and Robertson, op. cit., 179; Lane, pl. 24b; Pfuhl, fig. 59; Rumpf, pl. 6/7.
68. (Ch. I n. 24)
   Corinthian alabastron, Jason and serpent (?). 625/600. Bonn, Inv. 860.
   Ref: Greifenhagen, *A.A.*, 51 (1936), 343, figs. 6-7.
69. (Ch. I n. 24)
   Corinthian column-krater, banquet of Eurytos; suicide of Ajax. 625/600. From Caere. Paris, Louvre E 635.
   Ref: *NC.* no. 780; Pfuhl, fig. 176; Rumpf, pl. 13/6; *Enc. Phot.*, 270-3.
70. (Ch. II n. 76)
   Corinthian aryballos, flute-player and dancers. 600/575. From Corinth. Corinth (1954).
   Ref: M.C. and C.A. Roebuck, *Hesperia*, 24 (1955), 158.

71. (Ch. II n. 76)
Corinthian plaque (Timonidas), hunter. 600/575. From Corinth.
Berlin F 846.
Ref: *NC.* 104; Pfuhl, fig. 182; Rumpf, pl. 13/8 (cf. p. 52 on date).

72. (Ch. II n. 73; III n. 37; IV n. 6, 8)
Corinthian bottle (Timonidas), Achilles and Troilos. 600/575. From
Kleonai. Athens, N.M. 277.
Ref: *NC.* no. 1072; Pfuhl, fig. 174.

73 (Ch. I n. 24)
Corinthian column-krater, wedding of Helen. 600/575. From Italy.
New York 27.116.
Ref: *NC.* no. 1187; *N.Y. Handbook*, pl. 25b.

74. (Ch. I n. 42)
Corinthian kotyle, Muses and Apollo. 600/575. From Ithaca. Ithaca
39.
Ref: Robertson, *B.S.A.*, 43 (1948), 17, fig. 8.

75. (Ch. I n. 35)
Corinthian amphoriskos, bull taken in procession to sacrifice. 600/575.
From Greece. Oslo, Ethnographic Museum, Inv. 6909.
Ref: Eitrem, *A.E.*, 1952, 26.

76. (Ch. II n. 76; III n. 14)
Corinthian aryballos, dancer with phallos. 600/575. From Greece.
Oslo, Jensen Collection.
Ref: Seeberg, *Dagbladet*, 22 Feb. 1957; Webster, *W.S.*, 69 (1956),
110.

77. (Ch. III n. 16, 17, 20)
Corinthian amphoriskos, Return of Hephaistos. 600/575. Athens,
N.M. 664.
Ref: Payne, *NC.* no. 1073; *G.T.P.*, no. F 14.

78. (Ch. I n. 43; III n. 16)
Corinthian kotyle, padded dancers; Herakles and the hydra. 600/575.
Paris, Louvre CA 3004.
Ref: Amandry, *Mon. Piot*, 41 (1944), 23 ff.; *G.T.P.*, no. F 12.

79. (Ch. III n. 17; fig. 11)
Corinthian moulded vase, squatting dancer in hairy chiton and boots.
600/575. Dunedin 48.187.
Ref: Anderson pl. 4.

80. (Ch. I n. 24; IV n. 7)
Corinthian amphora, Perseus and Andromeda. 575/50. From Caere.
Berlin 1652.
Ref: *NC.* no. 1431; Pfuhl, fig. 190.

81. (Ch. I n. 43)
Corinthian hydria, Achilles mourned by sea-nymphs. 575/50. From
Caere. Paris, Louvre E 643.
Ref: *N.C.* no. 1446; Buschor, *Gr. Vasen*, fig. 79.

82. (Ch. I n. 43)
Corinthian column-krater, Sack of Troy. 575/50. From Delphi.
Delphi Museum.
Ref: *NC.* no. 1453.

83. (Ch. I n. 24; IV n. 11, 12)
Corinthian column-krater, A. Departure of Amphiaraos, B. Funeral
Games of Pelias. 575/50. From Caere. Berlin 1655.
Ref: *NC.* no. 1471; Pfuhl, fig. 179.

84. (Ch. I n. 24)
Corinthian column-krater, Odysseus' embassy to Troy. 575/50. Naples
(Astarita).
Ref: Beazley, *P.B.A.*, 43 (1957), 233 f.

85. (Ch. II n. 76; IV n. 7)
Laconian kylix, Arkesilas of Cyrene. 565/50. From Vulci. Paris, Cab.
Med. 4899.
Ref: Lane, *B.S.A.*, 34 (1934), 140 no. 1, 161; Shefton, *B.S.A.*, 49
(1954), 301 no. 16; Pfuhl, fig. 193; Rumpf, pl. 14/6.

86. (Ch. III n. 20)
Laconian kylix, Return of Hephaistos. 570/60. From Ialysos. Rhodes
10.711.
Ref: Shefton, 301, no. 3; Lane, 130 no. 5.

87. (Ch. II n. 74; fig. 9)
Chalkidian column-krater, Helen and Paris, Andromache and
Hektor. 540/30. From Vulci. Würzburg 315.
Ref: Rumpf, *Chalkidische Vasen*, no. 14.

3. CYCLADES

88. (Ch. I n. 52; II n. 31; IV n. 8; fig. 2)
Parian amphora, deer. 660/50. Stockholm, N.M. 1.
Ref: Rumpf, pl. 6/3; Brock, *B.S.A.*, 44 (1949), 80.

89. (Ch. I n. 38; II n. 72; IV n. 11; fig. 4)
Melian amphora, warriors and their mothers; Apollo arriving in
Delos. 660/50. From Melos. Athens, N.M. 911.
Ref: Pfuhl, fig. 108; Richter, fig. 49; Brock, loc. cit.

90. (Ch. I n. 24)
Naxian amphora, Aphrodite and Ares. 650 c. From Naxos. Athens,
N.M.
Ref: Karuzos, *J.d.I.*, 52 (1937), 177; Rumpf, pl. 6/6; Brock, loc. cit.

91. (Ch. I n. 45)
Melian amphora, Hermes and woman; Herakles and Deianira.
650/20. From Melos. Athens, N.M. 354.
Ref: Pfuhl, fig. 109-10; Richter, fig. 50; Rumpf, pl. 11/1.

4. ASIA MINOR

92. (Ch. I n. 27)
Rhodian plate, Menelaos and Hektor fight for the body of Euphorbos.
600/575. From Rhodes. London, British Museum A 749.
Ref: Lane, fig. 20a; Richter, fig. 76; Rumpf, pl. 7/4.

93. (Ch. I n. 28; III n. 28)
Rhodian plate, Gorgon-headed queen of beasts. 600/575. From
Rhodes. London, British Museum A 748.
Ref: *G.T.P.*, no. F 24.

94. (Ch. III n. 13)
Klazomenian amphora fragments, vintage; satyrs and ship-car.
550 c. From Karnak. Oxford 1924. 264.
Ref: *C.V.* II, pl. 10, 24; Boardman, *J.H.S.*, 78 (1958), pl. 1.

95. (Ch. II n. 38; III n. 20)
Fikellura amphoriskos, Dionysos and Ares. 525/500. From Rhodes.
Rhodes 12396.
Ref: Cook, *B.S.A.*, 34 (1934), 47, pl. 12.

96. (Ch. I n. 26; IV n. 8)
Caeretan hydria, Hermes and Apollo's oxen; Eos and Kephalos.
540/20. From Etruria. Paris, Louvre E 702.
Ref: Hemelrijk, *de Caeretaanse hydriae*, no. 3; *J.H.S.*, 48 (1928), pl.
13-14; Rumpf, pl. 18/3; Yalouris, *E.A.*, 1953-4, 173.

97. (Ch. III n. 20)
Caeretan hydria, Return of Hephaistos; satyr and maenad (bis).
540/20. From Etruria. Vienna 3577.
Ref: Hemelrijk, no. 4, cf. no. 9.

98. (Ch. I n. 47; fig. 15)
Caeretan hydria, boy between two horses. 540/20. Dunedin 53. 61.
Ref: Anderson, pl. 15; Anderson, *J.H.S.*, 75 (1955), 1 f.; Hemelrijk,
no. 15.

99. (Ch. I n. 26)
Caeretan hydria, Griffin and Arimaspian; satyr and maenad (bis).
540/20. From Etruria. London, British Museum 1923. 4-19. I.
Ref: Hemelrijk, no. 18; *J.H.S.*, 48 (1928), pl. 11, 12; Rumpf, pl. 18/4.

100. (Ch. I n. 26)
Caeretan hydria, Embassy to Achilles. 540/20. From Etruria. Paris,
Louvre.
Ref: Hemelrijk, no. 21; Pottier, *Mon. Piot*, 1933, 67.

101. (Ch. IV n. 10)
Caeretan hydria, Herakles and Busiris. 540/20. From Etruria. Vienna
3576.
Ref: Hemelrijk, no. 24; Pfuhl, fig. 152-3; Richter, fig. 211.

5. ITALY

102. (Ch. I n. 23)

Etruscan krater, Odysseus and Polyphemos; sea battle. 650 c. From Caere. Rome, Conservatori.

Ref: Pfuhl, fig. 64-5; Rumpf, pl. 6/1; Schweitzer, *R.M.* 60/61 (1953/4), 78 f.

103. (Ch. III n. 20)

Campana dinos, Return of Hephaistos. 540/25. From ? Italy. Louvre, Campana 10.233.

Ref: Villard, *Mon. Piot*, 43 (1946), 33 f.; Cook, *B.S.A.* 47 (1952), 150.

Index

References for individual works of art will be found in the List of Monuments. This index includes Museums, Sculpture, Vases with references to the numbers in the List of Monuments. For all other entries references are to pages of the text and notes.

Fig. 1

Fig. 2

Fig. 3

Fig. 4

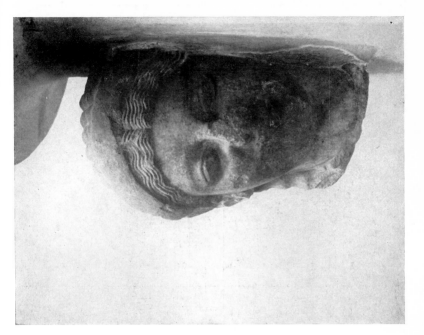

Fig. 6

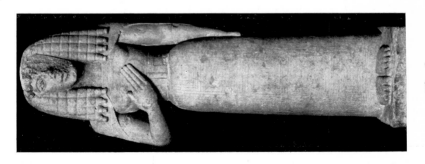

Fig. 5

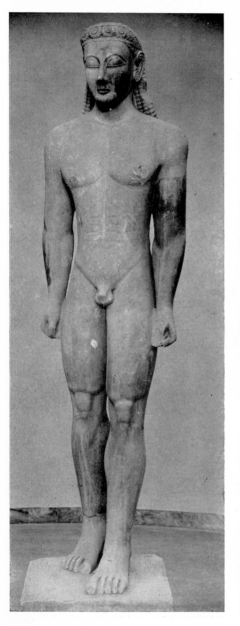

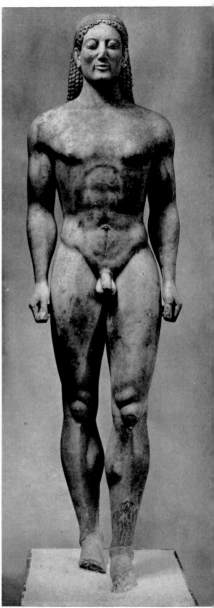

Fig. 7   Fig. 8

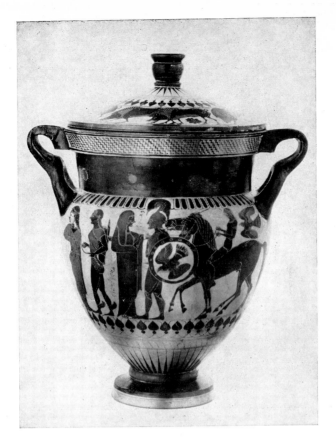

Fig. 9

Fig. 10

Fig. 14

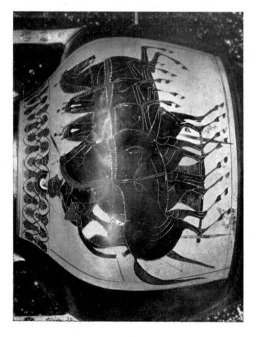

Fig. 13

Fig. 15

1